OpenStep™ for Enterprises

Nancy Craighill

Wiley Computer Publishing

John Wiley & Sons, Inc.
New York • Chichester • Brisbane • Toronto • Singapore • Weinheim

Publisher: Katherine Schowalter
Editor: Marjorie Spencer
Managing Editor: Frank Grazioli
Electronic Products Associate Editor: Mike Green
Text Design & Composition: Benchmark Productions, Inc.

All diagrams were created with DIAGRAM!2 by Lighthouse Design, Ltd.

This text is printed on acid-free paper.

This publication is designed to provide accurate and authoritative information in regard to the subject matter covered. It is sold with the understanding that the publisher is not engaged in rendering legal, accounting, or other professional service. If legal advice or other expert assistance is required, the services of a competent professional person should be sought.

Library of Congress Cataloging-in-Publication Data:
Craighill, Nancy, 1962-
    OpenStep for enterprises / Nancy Craighill
        p.cm
    Includes bibliographical references (p.).
    ISBN 0-471-30859-5 (paper : alk. paper)
    1. Applicaton software--Development. 2. OpenStep. I. Title
QA 76.76.A65C73 1996
005.2--dc20   96-17988
                                                         CIP

ISBN 0-471-30859-5
Printed in the United States of America
10 9 8 7 6 5 4 3 2 1

About the Author

Nancy Craighill is currently an independent software consultant and sometimes technical writer. At SRI International she used Objective-C and other Stepstone products to develop command and control systems for the U.S. Army. At the Stepstone Corporation she developed a 2D graphics class library, and authored the Objective-C column for the Journal of Object-Oriented Programming (JOOP). At Sony Electronics, Inc., she prototyped two high-end video editing systems. The first system was implemented in C++, X Windows, and Motif, and the second was implemented in NEXTSTEP. Recently she freelanced as a technical writer for NeXT Software, and wrote portions of NeXT's *OpenStep Reference Manual*. She also contributed chapters to other books: *Computer Graphics through Object-Oriented Programming* (published by John Wiley & Sons), and *Applications in Object-Oriented Programming* (published by Addison-Wesley).

To Sean and Lina

Acknowledgments

Thanks to NeXT Software for creating OpenStep, something worth writing about. NeXT staff answered many questions, especially Blaine Garst and the whole Technical Publications Department. Ron Hayden provided the opportunity for me to work with his talented staff and supported this book project in ways too numerous to mention. However, special thanks goes to Greg Wilson who lent me his equipment, schlepped my computer around, and even jumped my car in the pouring rain.

Thanks to Ivar Jacobson for creating the Jacobson Method (OOSE) and those indispensable interaction diagrams. Other Rational Software staff made individual contributions. Sten Jacobson and Haakan Dyrhage reviewed the analysis and design chapters, and Doug Earl provided expertise on the Booch Notation.

A special mention goes to my many reviewers. Vicki de Mey, Martin Fong, Bill Hunt, Randy Knolle, and Hemang Shukla provided thoughtful reviews and criticisms of the first draft. Dave Ciemiewicz, Henry McGilton, and Robert Nielson made excellent suggestions on the final draft. Henry McGilton also contributed immensely to the book design. Brad Cox and Kent Beck contributed to the philosophical direction of the book.

Thanks to John Wiley & Sons for their patience as circumstances beyond our control stretched this project from one to three years long. At first the topic was NEXTSTEP; then later it became OpenStep. Since the manuscript depended highly on the software, it became impossible to predict when the book might be published. Ironically, the release date of OpenStep for Windows coincided with the birth of my second child.

I couldn't have completed this project without the support from my family, especially my husband Earl for his never ending faith and encouragement. And last but certainly not least, my father Ernst Knolle and other family members for providing many months of day care.

Contents

vi   Contents

Figures

Tables

Preface

Goals

OpenStep is the premier object-oriented (OO)[†] development environment now available on Microsoft Windows, Sun Solaris and NeXT Mach platforms. OpenStep is not just a product, as in *OpenStep for Windows* sold by NeXT, but a specification of reusable classes called *frameworks*. Since it is an open standard, any software manufacture can provide an implementation of OpenStep. OpenStep is not new; it is proven technology that evolved from NeXT's original NEXTSTEP programming environment for Mach which has shipped since 1989.

For software developers OpenStep provides:

❑   *Objective-C*, a powerful hybrid OO language,
❑   *Interface Builder* for building user interfaces,
❑   *Project Builder* for organizing files, compiling and debugging code,
❑   *Foundation Kit* and *Application Kit*, several frameworks for quickly constructing those custom applications.

Support for *Distributed Objects*, the ability to send messages between processes, is implemented as an extension to the Objective-C language and through Foundation Kit classes. NeXT has ported its Distributed Objects to other platforms, such as HP-UX, and now supports interoperability with Microsoft OLE/COM objects and OMG CORBA implementations. Thus, your OpenStep objects can communicate with objects across heterogeneous platforms. In addition, an add-on product from NeXT, called *Enterprise Objects Framework (EOF)*, provides object persistency using traditional databases. All of these tools are the key to developing exciting new applications, such as hypermedia, groupware, and authoring tools.

---

† To save a couple of trees, "object-oriented" is abbreviated as "OO" throughout this book.

xvii

However, simply learning the OpenStep development tools does not ensure success with OO technology. Yes, you can quickly build custom applications, but without understanding the process of OO development and using proven methods of approach, the nifty user interface you create may just be a nice wrapper around the same old "spaghetti" code with the same old maintenance problems.

Perhaps the first application you develop using OpenStep is successful, but now that it is in use by real customers you are overwhelmed with problem reports and requests for enhancements and wondering if starting from scratch would be easier. Or, your first application was received well within the company, and now your organization wants to adopt the technology enterprise-wide, but you're having difficulty scaling up your custom application to meet these new demands.

At this point, you might blame the environment and technology (it hasn't lived up to your expectations) without realizing that the environment is only one ingredient for successful OO development. Using OpenStep for serious software development on a large scale requires more understanding of the OO development process.

The goal of this book is to help you succeed in using OpenStep, not just for one application, but enterprise-wide, by building suites of interoperable applications. OO development on a large scale requires not only new tools, but a new philosophy about software development, new management style, and an underlying architecture that supports interoperability. Specifically, the goals of this book are:

❏   Introduce the OO Software Development Life Cycle and different management styles.
❏   Teach OO analysis and design methods, notations, and techniques.
❏   Teach OpenStep development tools and frameworks.
❏   Provide deeper understanding and appreciation of Objective-C.
❏   Demonstrate the power of Distributed Objects by focusing on problems faced when designing client-server applications.

This book contains real design and code examples by developing a theme application, called *Cards*, throughout. The application is an analysis tool, a computerization of CRC or modelling cards, that has aspects of both hypermedia and groupware. The design and implementation of Cards is non-trivial, making it ideal for teaching advanced features of OpenStep. Since Cards is an analysis tool, you can also use it when developing your own applications. The complete source code is provided on the enclosed disk so you can extend it to meet your needs.

By covering the entire OO development process and advanced features of OpenStep, this book gives you all the necessary skills to succeed with reuse in your organization and build interoperable systems suitable for the new information age.

Audience

This book is suitable for computer professionals, program managers, and students. Specific sections of the book address the process of OO development and new management techniques. It contains in-depth design and programming examples using OpenStep. Chapter 6—*Implementation*, written in tutorial style, and the source code on the enclosed disk could be used in a software engineering course.

Organization

Chapter 1—*Introduction* provides "The Big Picture" of what is taking place in the software industry today and where it is headed. It also explains why OO technology in general, and OpenStep in particular, is the fastest vehicle to developing next generation software.

Chapters immediately following Chapter 1 explain the process of OO development including the OO life cycle and iteration strategies, teach the Jacobson OO analysis and design method, and apply the Booch notation. Chapter 5—*Design* introduces OpenStep classes and reusable designs called mechanisms. Chapter 6—*Implementation* teaches Open-Step development tools, frameworks, and more mechanisms. You can implement your own version of the example application while reading this chapter.

The final chapter, Chapter 7—*Distributed Objects*, ties it all together. It's not only a goal for large enterprises to use Distributed Objects. Distributed applications, including client-server applications, require more attention to design—you can't just hack a distributed application together and expect it to interoperate. OO methods and notations can really help to understand the complexity of distributed applications, and applying these techniques produces better results.

The appendices also contain important information:

❑ Appendix A—*A Laboratory For Teaching OO Thinking* contains a reprint of the Beck and Cunningham paper that is used as the requirements specification for the Cards application.

❑ Appendix B—*Objective-C* contains a brief introduction to the language and syntax while also explaining how messaging in Objective-C works.

❑ Appendix C—*Booch Lite* contains a description of the Booch Notation with adaptations for Objective-C and Distributed Objects.

❑ Appendix D—*Class Specifications* contains specifications for principle Cards classes. Use this appendix as a reference when examining the source code and extending the application.

❑ Appendix E—*Further Reading* contains references to additional information.

Using the Book

Chapter 1 provides the background and rationale for why this technology is so important. Chapter 2 may be skipped if you are already versed in OO programming concepts. Chapter 3, Chapter 4, and Chapter 5, are best read in succession and provide the foundation for the examples in the rest of the book. Chapter 6 covers the single user, single process version of Cards. Chapter 7 adds support for groupware, and assumes familiarity with the Cards design, Objective-C and Booch notation, and therefore should be read last. Read Appendix B if you are unfamiliar with the language or want to understand how it works. Be sure to read Appendix C if you are unfamiliar with the Booch Notation before reading Chapter 5.

Conventions

This book is after all a programming book and contains many references to programming "things," often OpenStep specific. Therefore it is worth mentioning some conventions used in this book.

Bold denotes words or characters that are to be taken literally. Specifically, method names, instance variables, other local and global variables, and types will appear in **bold**. For example, Objective-C method names such as **setTitle:**, and types such as **id** and **int** appear in **bold**. On the other hand, classes, protocols, categories, notifications and exceptions will not be emphasized but always appear capitalized, as is the OpenStep convention.

If unspecified, a method name is always assumed to be an instance method, otherwise the statement will be qualified as in "the **init** class method."

To improve the legibility of this book, words are sometimes coined from class and method names. For example, the term *views* refers to instances of NSView and the phrase "an object is released" implies that an object was sent the **release** message.

Introduction

The ever increasing demand for software has created what is known as the "software crisis."[†] This book expands the theme that OO technology, in particular OpenStep, is one part of the solution to this crisis. However, just learning new OO programming tools is not enough to succeed within an enterprise. OO technology requires new approaches to managing software development, new analysis and design methods, and new notations. Also, Distributed Objects has the potential to revolutionize the way software is packaged—expanding software reuse from enterprise to industry-wide. The "information super highway" will soon be in place. Organizations wishing to be at the forefront of this new "information age" must have strategies for delivering applications and services that interoperate over large networks.

The Software Crisis

In general, software always seems to lag behind hardware. Every time hardware processors become faster, the next generation of software systems just consume more processor and memory resources so that the end user barely notices any performance improvements. In fact, most users have to upgrade their hardware simply to run the latest version of their favorite software packages which seem to grow exponentially in size and processor requirements. Sure there are some new features, but doesn't the user deserve more, especially after investing in new hardware?

So who's to blame for creating "kitchen sink" applications that become inefficient resource hogs? Software managers blame programmers for creating "spaghetti code" that is too difficult to maintain and enhance.

---

† The term "software crisis" was first coined by a Working Conference on Software Engineering, sponsored by the NATO Science Committee in Garmish, Germany, in 1968.

Such a manager might exclaim: "Programmers aren't as skilled as in the pioneer days, when computers had 32K memory. Today, programmers opt for the quickest solution, not the most optimal, just to get the job done."

The typical response from the programmer is to blame managers for demanding too much, creating unreasonable schedules that allow no time for design, and then always changing and adding features at the last minute. And, to make matters worse, programmers rarely get a chance to rewrite their code once it is released, since after that they are entirely consumed with enhancements, maintenance, and porting activities. No wonder quality-conscious programmers seem to change jobs often.

As Brad Cox writes in *Object-Oriented Programming: An Evolutionary Approach*:

> *We're already face to face with the software crisis—the awareness that ambitious software systems are generally too expensive, of insufficient quality, hard to schedule reliably, and nearly impossible to manage.*

Perhaps in the pioneer days software development was an art form, but today we realize that it should be an engineering discipline requiring methods of approach and techniques for long term success.

A Brief History

First there was structured design and programming; now OO technology is touted as the solution to this crisis. OO technology is not just a new programming language, but also a design discipline that has matured over the past quarter century to improve reusability, extensibility, and maintainability of software.

At first OO programming environments, such as Smalltalk, were designed for individual and somewhat novice programmers (for example, scientists and geologist) to better abstract their application models, customize existing applications, and quickly create sophisticated graphical user interfaces (GUIs). See *Introducing Object-Oriented Technology into an Organization* by Adele Goldberg and Kenneth Rubin.

Early Smalltalk systems assumed a single user–single workstation configuration. Partly because of this, OO programming was considered research technology, good for prototyping but not suitable for production code. However, in the late seventies and early eighties, hybrid OO programming languages such as LOOPS and Flavors for LISP, Object Pascal, Objective-C, and C++ for C, and new languages, such as Eiffel, were developed that together helped OO programming gain a wider acceptance by mainstream programmers. In recent years, even Smalltalk has had a surge of popularity and is now being used on serious product development. With endorsements from every major software manufacturer, OO technology is now widely accepted in the industry (according to the March 1995 *Object-Oriented Strategies* newsletter, OO tool sales tripled from 1991 to 1994). There is even talk of an Objective-COBOL language!

In just the past five years, numerous books have been published on OO analysis and design methods. In fact, in 1994 the Object Management Group (OMG) documented over twenty different OO methods from around the world. Other new books address OO project management, and Jacobson has even applied OO concepts to business engineering. See Appendix E—*Further Reading*.

From a corporate point of view, OO programming makes a great deal of sense. OO programming improves the overall quality of software products (they are more reliable, portable, and maintainable) and, after the initial investment, considerably reduces the time required to get products to market. Combined with advances in network computing (making it now feasible to share software components in a large organization), OO programming is now being adopted enterprise-wide. Organizations are realizing that OO technology is not just for programmers—it will even improve the competitiveness of the entire organization.

The Vision

In the mid eighties, Cox (inventor of Objective-C) envisioned a software revolution similar to the industrial revolution two hundred years ago that transformed firearm cottage industries into manufacturers of standard interchangeable parts. Similarly, software could be built from reusable, interchangeable, and most importantly reliable components.[†]

---

† M.D. McIlroy expressed similar views at the Software Engineering conference sponsored by the NATO Science Committee in Garmish, Germany, 1968.

Imagine putting together a software system much like putting together a stereo sound system—by buying software components off the shelf and plugging them together. In this way, OO programming was expected to revolutionize software engineering by dividing software manufacturing into part suppliers and part assemblers.

So, decades later, why hasn't the software revolution happened as envisioned? The dream of a software component warehouse may remain in the hearts of many software engineers. Although there are frameworks for constructing user interfaces and providing basic foundation classes (for example, collections, lists, trees, etc.), you can't build your "stereo system" without building a plenitude of custom objects.

Perhaps reuse in the form of software component warehouses may never happen. As Goldberg and Rubin point out, vendors need to build novel systems to compete, which is difficult to do from standard components. Also, vendors are reluctant to sell their proprietary objects, since supplying a class library reveals the entire OO design (the classes, inheritance, and methods), possibly giving away trade secrets. Goldberg and Rubin make this observation:

> ...software manufacturers, in particular object-oriented ones, acknowledge that their skills are demonstrated by the external specifications—coding is straight forward and manufacturing is free.

Also, software reuse is far from easy. Reuse skills need to evolve before marketing components becomes an issue. Organizations need to stop looking for a panacea from OO vendors (expecting to buy every component off-the-shelf). After all, if you can't achieve software reuse within your organization where you have complete control, how can you expect to achieve software reuse industry-wide? For this reason, this book focuses on software reuse within the enterprise.

OO programming will not make a great impact on an organization by simply using OO programming tools in isolated groups. The key to successfully applying this technology within an organization is to build an infrastructure that promotes software reuse *throughout* the organization. Sure, selecting OpenStep is a big step towards success, but there needs to be equal emphasis on managing the development process, applying methods, adopting notations, and even organizational change if necessary.

Organizations should no longer build one monolithic product for a single marketplace. Instead, they need to identify application domains and build reusable components that can be used by a range of applications. This strategy gives organizations a competitive edge by allowing them to better prepare for long product life cycles and quickly respond to parallel target markets and changing market needs.

Perhaps when organizations successfully practice reuse, they will be able to specify components and begin to contract out their development. Contractors who have many clients will then be able to identify the common needs of different organizations and actually begin to produce Software-ICs as Cox envisioned. Cox coined the term *Software-IC* to emphasize the similarity with an integrated silicon chip which revolutionized the hardware industry. Most likely, these early Software-ICs will be application-domain specific, not intended for general consumption, and very expensive.

This might work well for niche markets like high finance, but it's not an industry-wide software revolution, is it?

After having co-founded a company to market Software-ICs with disappointing results, Cox switched focus from supplying tools, now believing that the problem is with the revenue collection mechanisms for software (see articles *Testing Object-Oriented Components: A Human-centric Perspective* and *No Silver Bullet Revisited* by Brad Cox). The premise is that suppliers need more incentive and more money to manufacture components.

Cox suggests we use *superdistribution*, creating "meterware." Instead of selling copies of software, we should make software easily available and create revenue by the number of times it is used. The assumption is that software manufacturers would produce more revenue with meterware since it prevents software pirating (you can't copy software you don't have). This approach may also be better for the consumer, since the free market will ensure competitive pricing and quality. The consumer might pay very little for each incremental use, and can quit using the software at any time. Why pay for software you don't use? Before superdistribution can happen, the software revolution has one more battle to win.

Impact of Distributed Objects

Not only does software lag behind hardware, but application software lags considerably behind advances in networking. Just because users can share application documents via networks, doesn't make an application network-aware. Also, most systems that claim to be groupware are really just modeled after electronic mail and support no real-time collaboration between users. With the expectations of the information super highway and interactive TV, groupware and hypermedia information systems should be a booming business in the next decade. The overnight success of the World Wide Web is proof of the high demand for such systems. In the near future, vendors must deliver interoperable applications that take full advantage of a distributed computing environment to survive.

Distributed Objects is the technology that will overcome this hurdle. Distributed Objects takes reuse one step further by bringing the benefits of OO programming to the end user and changing the way we package applications. Distributed Objects enables diverse applications to communicate through defined object interfaces across heterogeneous environments. Applications are no longer monolithic; instead they are built using reusable components and *services*, other programs that offer a common service (for example, a video editor might use a morphing service). Services are programs that dynamically connect to applications at runtime; thus an application's capabilities are as much determined by design as by the runtime environment. Applications would then become frameworks, truly open systems, easily allowing end-user and third party extensions.

End-users would be happy because they can mix and match applications and services to meet their individual needs and budgets without being software experts. Vendors would be happy because they do not need to publish complete interfaces to their objects that might reveal proprietary designs. This gives vendors more incentive to market components.

Distributed Objects also impacts the business model for marketing software. New opportunities arise for small businesses to supply specialized add-on components to framework applications produced by large businesses. And, because Distributed Objects can reduce large monolithic programs into many cooperating processes, it's actually more feasible and profitable to market these components as meterware.

Distributed Objects is not just available in OpenStep; it is becoming an industry standard. OMG has over 130 company members dedicated to promoting not only reusable and portable software components but interoperability by standardizing OO interfaces. OMG's Common Object Request Broker Architecture (CORBA) is a standard specification for an Object Request Broker (ORB) with implementations provided by, for example, Sun, HP, IBM, and Digital. NeXT's Portable Distributed Objects (PDO) can interoperate with CORBA implementations and even Microsoft's Object Linking and Embedding (OLE)/Component Object Model (COM) objects (the other standard). Using Distributed Objects, your applications can communicate with applications across large networks on diverse platforms.

The OpenStep Advantage

So what does all this have to do with OpenStep? OpenStep is one of the most complete OO development environments on the market today and therefore the fastest vehicle to building next generation software systems—applications for the information age. The Distributed Objects system is elegant and easy to use—ideal for creating applications such as groupware and hypermedia featured in this book. The advantage that OpenStep has is that the Objective-C, and consequently the Distributed Objects, messaging model is dynamic, not static. This allows you to achieve real software reuse at every level, as this book illustrates.

For many of us, the information super highway is here today—the problem is that the software doesn't take full advantage of it yet.

OO Programming   2

This chapter describes the basic principles of OO programming and defines common terminology used throughout the book. It also addresses the differences between some OO languages such as Objective-C and C++.

Objective-C is the primary implementation language for OpenStep and, since it is a Smalltalk derivative, we use "classic" terminology borrowed from Smalltalk in this book (consistent with OpenStep documentation). Thus, terms like *member function*, which is C++ specific, are used only in the context of that programming language.

Although there are many different OO programming languages, the underlying principles of OO programming are the same: encapsulation, inheritance, and polymorphism. The premise is that these principles, combined with good design, will produce reusable, extensible, and maintainable code.

These OO programming principles and other features specific to Objective-C and C++ are described below. This chapter does not contain a complete description of Objective-C; see Appendix B—*Objective-C* for more details.

Encapsulation

An object *encapsulates* its data structures and algorithms by defining a public interface that specifies *what* an object does, not *how* it does it. Objects then communicate via *messages* without incurring interdependencies between object implementations. An OO program is essentially a network of objects with messages flowing between them. The goal is to design an object as a reusable, pluggable module within this network that can be improved or replaced without affecting the rest of the program.

9

So how does OO programming differ from procedural and structured programming? You can mimic OO programming in a procedural language such as C, for example. However, without OO language support maintaining a separation between data and operations on that data is very difficult. Also, procedures and functions ultimately limit your ability to reuse software. OO programming adds an abstraction layer above data and functions, hiding implementation details of objects so that they can be thought of only in terms of their behavior.

The first abstraction is a *class*, a template for creating object *instances* that specifies data called *instance variables*, and algorithms or routines that operate on the data called *methods*. The application then uses classes at runtime to create *instances*, objects that can receive and process messages at runtime. Note, a *message* tells an object what to do and a *method* implements that operation.

For example, Plane is a class with instance variables **fuel** and **weight**, and methods **takeOff** and **land**. **aPlane** is an instance of Plane that corresponds to a real-world plane that is sitting on the runway and has its own specific values for **fuel** and **weight** such as 1,000 gallons and 10 tons. Sending the **land** message to **aPlane** will execute its **land** method.

Because the class Plane is used to create instances, it is sometimes called a *factory object*. In Smalltalk and Objective-C, classes are also *objects* that can receive and process messages. Some languages allow *class variables* and *class methods* that pertain to factory objects only.

Inheritance

Inheritance facilitates reuse by abstracting common variables and methods into a *superclass* so that *subclasses* may inherit these characteristics. For example, we might create a subclass of Plane called Boeing747 which would inherit the **fuel** and **weight** instance variables and all the methods, but which may define additional variables and new methods as shown in Figure 2–1. The Boeing747 class may also change inherited behavior by *overriding* inherited methods (providing a different implementation). Software is reused because common code is not replicated in each subclass. Programmer productivity is improved because only additional variables, methods, and overridden methods, need to be defined in each subclass.

Figure 2–1   Plane class structure.

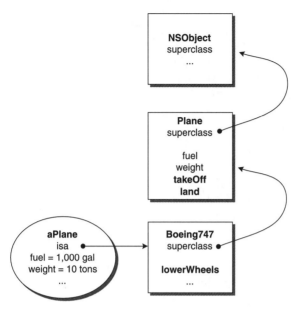

Some languages support both single and multiple inheritance, where *multiple inheritance* allows classes to inherit variables and methods from more than one class.

An *abstract superclass* or *abstract class* is a class whose sole purpose is to abstract common characteristics and behavior for its subclasses, and is never intended to have instances. The prime example of an abstract class in OpenStep is NSObject which all objects inherit from.

Polymorphism

Polymorphism is the ability to send the same messages to disparate types of objects. For example, the message **land** could be sent to an instance of Plane or an instance of Helicopter. Each class may define a **land** method even though Plane and Helicopter may have no common ancestors in the class hierarchy. In programming language terms, polymorphism means that each class has its own name space. This is an important feature of OO languages, since it allows simpler programming interfaces.

Variations

Encapsulation, inheritance, and polymorphism are the common features of every OO language. However, OO languages vary in their support for encapsulation and message passing. Some even introduce new ideas for software reuse. For example, protocols and categories, recently added to Objective-C, provide another dimension to sharing object interfaces without using inheritance. A more extreme example is the language called Self that replaces inheritance entirely with a new style of reuse called prototyping.

Most OO programming languages fall into one of two categories. *Class-based languages* include the family of Smalltalk-like and LISP-derived languages, which fully support dynamic binding (described below) and the notion of a factory object. On the other hand, *type-based languages*, such as C++, derive from Simula and its notion of abstract data types, but rely upon compile-time type checking. Type-based languages tend to be less flexible in implementing dynamic runtime behavior and have difficulty producing generic classes. However, type-based languages *may* have an edge when performance is critical.

When using OpenStep, you will primarily program in Objective-C, which is a class-based language. However, you can choose C++ as the base language instead of C to give the most variety, or simply to utilize existing C++ components. However, you should first understand the strengths and weaknesses of each language because it may impact your design.

Dynamic Binding

Dynamic binding is the ability to map a message to an implementation or method at runtime. For example, the OpenStep NSArray class is a collection of arbitrary objects; it can contain instances of entirely different classes. The types of objects contained in the array are not defined until runtime; therefore, messages sent to those objects are dynamically bound at runtime.

For example, suppose an instance of NSArray contains instances of Plane, Helicopter, and SpaceShip, where each understands the message **land**. To make all elements in the collection land themselves, we simply send **land** to each element and let the Objective-C runtime system decide which **land** method implementation to execute:

```
[listOfFlyingThings makeObjectsPerform:@selector(land)];
```

NSArray's **makeObjectsPerform:** method sends the message specified as the argument to all objects in its array.

C++ is a type-based language and does not support dynamic binding. Templates in C++ can be used to create array classes, each containing different types of objects, but it can't be used to create an array containing arbitrary types of objects (objects that do not inherit from the same superclass).

Dynamic Typing

Languages that support dynamic binding will also support dynamic typing. *Dynamic typing* is the ability to wait until runtime to determine the class of an object. In contrast, *static typing* requires that the object type be declared at compile-time. Objective-C supports both dynamic and static typing whereas C++ supports only static typing. For example, in Objective-C a dynamically typed object is declared as type **id**, otherwise the class name is used, as in:

```
id          aPlane;
Boeing747   *the747;
```

Late Binding

In C++, every object does not need to be exactly typed; an object can be typed to any class it inherits from. For example, if class B inherits from class A, an instance of class B may be passed as an argument to a member function typed as class A. This is called *late binding* because the exact type is determined at runtime. Although somewhat "dynamic," late binding is not to be confused with dynamic binding. Late binding still imposes strict compile-time type checking, whereas dynamic binding is completely unrestricted.

Dynamic Loading

Dynamic loading is the ability to add new classes and objects to a program as it is running. Dynamic loading makes applications extensible by enabling third parties to add and customize them by simply publishing an interface. For example, OpenStep's Graphical User Interface (GUI) builder called *Interface Builder* can dynamically load custom palettes and inspectors you create.

The dynamic features of an OO language enable programmers to create generic classes that can be more reusable than type-specific classes. For example, code written today can send messages to objects not yet invented simply by agreeing on common messages, not data types. Much of the flexibility and power of Interface Builder, and OpenStep in general, is credited to the dynamic features of Objective-C. For more details on how messaging works in Objective-C, see Appendix B.

Summary

This chapter described OO programming concepts and defined common terminology:

❑   *Encapsulation* hides object implementation details by defining a public interface that specifies what an object does, not how it does it.

❑   Objects then send *messages* to each other without incurring interdependencies between object implementations.

❑   A *class* is a template for creating object *instances*. The class data is called *instance variables* and the algorithms or routines are called *methods*.

❑   A *message* tells an object what to do and a *method* implements it.

❑   Classes that also respond to messages are called *factory objects*. Variables and methods that pertain to factory objects are called *class variables* and *class methods*.

❑   *Object* generally refers to any entity that can receive and process messages.

❑   *Inheritance* abstracts common variables and methods into a superclass that subclasses may inherit.

❏   *Multiple inheritance* allows classes to inherit variables and methods from more than one class.

❏   *Polymorphism* is the ability to send the same message to objects belonging to distinctly different classes.

❏   *Dynamic binding* maps messages to methods at runtime, not compile-time.

❏   *Dynamic typing* is the ability to wait until runtime to determine the class of an object.

❏   *Static typing* requires that the object type be declared at run time.

❏   *Late binding* allows an object to be typed as a superclass.

❏   *Dynamic loading* is the ability to add new classes and objects to a program as it is running.

Programming languages can be characterized as either class-based or type-based. *Class-based* languages support dynamic binding and the notion of a factory object. *Type-based* languages support abstract data types, but rely upon compile-time type checking. Objective-C is a class-based language and C++ is a type-based language. Both languages are available when using OpenStep but understanding the strengths and weaknesses of each language is important to your design.

The Process

3

The process of developing software is modeled by a *life cycle* that outlines the stages of development and their sequence. The life cycle provides structure for project management and is an important aid to the entire development team. Most large software projects use some form of a life cycle—even ad-hoc projects that don't realize there is a life cycle. However, traditional life cycles ultimately fail because they are really just a defense strategy against change, which is a normal and very reasonable characteristic of software development. In contrast, OO technology is designed to better adapt to change and therefore requires a new approach to the life cycle as well. The OO life cycle presented in this chapter actually promotes positive change through iteration, improving the overall quality of the end product, and ultimately making the customer happy.

The ideas presented in this chapter are not new. The problems with traditional approaches to software development are well documented, and the OO life cycle and iteration strategies described here are generally accepted. In fact, the OMG document entitled *Object Analysis and Design, Volume 1: Reference Model* concurs that:

> *Incremental, additive, non-staged, risk-managed development is a practical proposition for object-oriented development.*

Another goal of this chapter is to translate this technical jargon into layman's terms.

This chapter is beneficial to developers and managers alike, especially when attempting to apply OO technology enterprise-wide. Ambitious projects need more structure and direction to succeed, but even small projects benefit from following a life cycle. Even if steps are skipped, the path from beginning to end is the same.

Problems with Waterfall Life Cycle

The traditional *waterfall life cycle* shown in Figure 3–1 (taken from *Object-Oriented Design with Applications* by Grady Booch) dictates that each stage of development be carried out in strict sequence. Often the outputs from each stage are documented in great detail and "signed off" by all parties, including the customer. This approach is popular because it appears to be easy to manage, costs seem controllable or at least accountable, and, in large organizations where each stage is conducted by a different group, it may be necessary. The waterfall life cycle is, however, very rigid; it does not allow for change and, in fact, discourages change.

Figure 3–1   Waterfall Life Cycle.

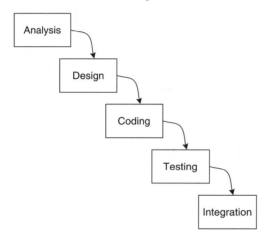

In addition, the waterfall life cycle is considered high risk because nothing tangible, besides paper, is produced until the end. Unfortunately, by managing the "paper," managers think they are managing the project. Consequently, projects most often suffer from the "90 percent done" syndrome as described by Edward Yourdon in *Object-Oriented Systems Design*:

> *... the project team may report to its manager, "We just finished drawing all the object diagrams with our CASE tool, boss, and they look real good! We think we're 90 percent done—all that's left is a simple matter of programming!"*

Invariably the effort to implement a working system has been grossly underestimated, and a big scramble begins to finish the system on time.

Unfortunately, it will be too late to correct design flaws discovered during implementation or to allow any customer feedback. Perhaps the requirements specification is met, but customer is nevertheless unhappy with the results. Even worse, the system may be riddled with bugs when delivered and is completely unusable. Wouldn't the customer have been happier if some features were omitted but the system was at least operational?

Consequently, the product is not marketable or the customer does not fund follow-on projects. The software change that was so desperately avoided at the onset is just postponed to the maintenance stage which is now flooded with problem reports and requests for enhancements. It's no surprise that eighty percent of the typical project life cycle is spent in maintenance!

The result is that we end up producing very large "kitchen sink" applications that are maintained forever by hackers. As Cox points out in *Object Oriented Programming: An Evolutionary Approach*, "hacking" is just uncontrolled change. Maintaining these systems can be all-consuming, stifling innovation in large companies and literally killing small companies. In extreme cases, we end up avoiding the maintenance nightmare altogether by re-implementing the system from scratch with each release. No wonder software is so expensive to build!

The fact is change is inevitable. Requirements change because the problem domain is rarely well understood at the onset of a project by both developers and customers. The environment around software constantly changes, especially in a distributed system. Even if your environment doesn't change, your knowledge of it might. Consequently, some software systems need to be constantly updated just to keep running.

Another difficulty with software development is that project milestones are often influenced more by the market than by how long the development will actually take. Therefore, managers are forced to commit to impossible deadlines and often unrealistic schedules to achieve all objectives. For example, a military contractor might cram development efforts between military exercises, and a commercial company might squeeze development efforts between trade conferences. Even if the deliverable is just a prototype, military exercises and yearly conferences have immovable deadlines that can wreak havoc on any software team attempting to deliver a complete system.

These unavoidable characteristics of the software industry make software development both challenging and exciting. Would we really have it any other way? Therefore, instead of fighting change, we need a better strategy to support evolutionary software development and phased deliverables. Ideally, maintenance as a separate activity would be virtually eliminated since enhancements and bug fixes are part of the normal evolution of software.

OO programming was designed precisely to reduce the impact of change on the entire system and improve extensibility. *Encapsulation* hides implementation details so you can easily locate and fix problems, and *inheritance* promotes reuse so you can easily make enhancements. However, just using OO programming during implementation will not fix the overall project problems mentioned above. In fact, if the management structure is not changed and new methods and notations adopted, team members will become even more frustrated because the promises of the "software revolution" brought about by OO technology will not be realized.

The OO Life Cycle

Early OO developers recognized the necessity for iteration in improving, understanding and completing the specifications of the problem domain. Therefore, the OO life cycle does not significantly alter the stages of development but instead allows multiple passes through the cycle, refining the OO model with each iteration, as well as producing a working prototype. The OO life cycle illustrated in Figure 3–2 is taken from *Object Analysis and Design, Volume 1: Reference Model*. All of the stages are similar to those that would appear in a waterfall life cycle except the first. The upward flowing arrows were added to illustrate iteration strategies discussed later in this chapter.

Figure 3–2   The OO Life Cycle.

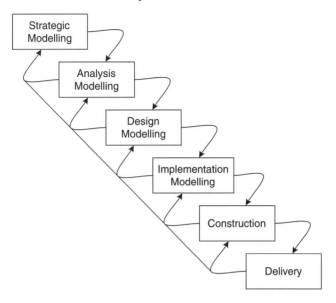

The *strategic modelling* stage is the process of developing a strategy for delivering current and future products. Specifically an organization needs to identify the reusable components, common services and interoperability requirements for the whole application domain, not just one product. This includes examining components from third parties if they exist.

Strategic modelling is important for OpenStep developers planning on using Distributed Objects. An application or product should no longer be considered one monolithic program, but a collection of applications and services that communicate via Distributed Objects.

The goal of *analysis modelling* is to obtain a complete understanding of the problem domain. The input to analysis may include any one of the following: a problem statement, detailed requirements specification, or dialogue with domain experts. Sometimes this activity includes discovering and documenting requirements. The outputs of analysis are the high-level objects and their relationships, and a description of the system behaviors in terms of these objects. Ideally, the analysis model is understandable by all (customers, managers, and developers alike), establishes the terminology used throughout the project, and provides a good foundation for design.

OMG separates design into *design modelling* and *implementation modelling;* one stage focuses on the external view and the other on the internal view of application objects. For example, design modelling might produce specifications of the public operations and interfaces, whereas implementation modelling might produce complete object specifications and groupings of objects into software modules.

However, not all OO analysis/design methods agree with this exact separation. In fact, the method used in this book, the Jacobson Method, makes a more important distinction between the part of the design that is implementation environment independent and dependent, on the premise that it is the implementation environment that most often changes. Therefore, at this level of discussion, we simply consider these all steps of *design*.

During *design,* the emphasis shifts from *what* to *how* by refining the analysis models into a complete design and meeting all the computer imposed constraints of modularity, distribution, efficiency, quality, and so on. This includes a rigorous specification of the system architecture, as well as the objects and their interfaces. The design is best captured using a design notation (such as the Booch Notation for drawing process diagrams, object diagrams, and class hierarchy, and groups of classes into categories and modules).

Construction is the implementation of the design using the selected programming language and tools, and *delivery* is the release of the class libraries and/or applications.

It is also common to build a proof of concept prototype before doing anything else for the sole purpose of validating your ideas. Sometimes a prototype is required to win approval of a new project, especially if you're venturing into a new business area. Booch formalizes this step in *Object-Oriented Analysis and Design with Applications* and calls it *conceptualization* where the prototype produced is quick-and-dirty and unequivocally throw-away. Conceptualization is typically conducted by just a few individuals: for example, the visionary and a skilled programmer.

Note: *user interface design* is not considered a separate stage of development. The user interface is simply a collection of objects that act as an intermediary between the user and internal model objects. Therefore, user interface objects will be treated just like other objects; identified during analysis and refined during design.

The strength of the OO approach is a uniform object model that is developed throughout the life cycle. Thus, there is little translation, and therefore less chance of misinterpretation, of the output from one stage into the next. It is easy to verify that the implementation matches the design, the design matches the analysis, and so forth, since the same objects may appear at each level of abstraction. This "traceability" also makes OO CASE tools more powerful, since some of the translations can be automated (including some code generation).

Perhaps the sole disadvantage of the OO life cycle is that, because of the common object model, there's a fuzzy line between each stage which can sometimes make it difficult to decide when to go to the next stage. Along with the iteration strategies described below, this can make managing OO development challenging.

Iteration Strategies

Variations of this basic OO life cycle described above are in the iteration strategies used. OMG thoroughly documents all conceivable iteration strategies in *Object Analysis and Design: Volume 1: Reference Model*. The two most commonly used strategies for OO development are discussed here: rapid prototyping and incremental development.

Rapid prototyping is where the iteration cycles are fast and limited in scope solely for the purpose of better understanding the problem domain and soliciting customer feedback. In this case, the prototype code is completely thrown away; it is *not* production code. Rapid prototyping is typically followed by a more traditional development cycle, but may be followed by any other iteration strategy.

The problem with rapid prototyping is that it is difficult to know when to quit. Too often managers and customers alike are fooled into believing the system is nearly complete, even when it is printed in **bold** that the prototype will be thrown away. Also, programmers that invest a lot of time prototyping may be unwilling to throw away their own code. Hence, there is a danger that poor design decisions make their way into the end product. In fact, for this reason, Goldberg and Rubin, in *Introducing Object-Oriented Technology into an Organization*, suggest that different programmers be assigned to implement the actual production system. This makes a lot of sense since programmers that have a knack for hacking are not necessarily good designers, and vice versa. Some organizations take even more drastic actions like purposely using a different platform for the prototype. In one case, a visionary implemented his prototype in assembly language just so it could not be used to construct a real product!

In contrast, an *incremental development* strategy builds the system in small manageable increments producing a working "version" of the system at the end of each cycle. Ideally, each version should be operational and can also be used in limited production to solicit customer feedback. It is important to emphasize that although partially implemented, each version is still production quality and should not contain any "mock-ups" or "smoke and mirrors."

It is interesting to note that incremental development was not feasible in the past because the cost of integration was too high. Since a good OO design encapsulates data and methods into objects, it is easier to divide the problem space into groups of classes with well specified interfaces. Thus, integration of these components is substantially simplified.

In contrast to the waterfall life cycle, incremental development is low risk. It is an efficient use of time and resources, produces tangible results along the way, and allows time for important customer feedback. The "versions" can also be used by marketing as demos to potential customers and as deliverables for some of these immovable deadlines (for example, trade conferences), thus reducing the number of distractions from real development. Also, productivity is better measured since there is no confusion between perceived progress, as when managing "paper," and actual progress. Problems with the design and the performance of team members can be detected and thus corrected early on. Changes to the requirements can even be accommodated (for example, a competitor releases their product before yours and you must now shift focus to keep a market share).

As always, a hybrid approach is best. Often rapid prototyping is used very early in the project to flush out the user interface, or sometimes before a project is even funded just to demonstrate the proposed functionality. Rapid prototyping is practically a necessity during analysis modelling as an aid in discovering system behaviors. How much time is spent on rapid prototyping depends on your project. A good rule of thumb is to begin incremental development as soon as the first objects become solidified or once the design stage begins. Whatever you choose, don't attempt to conduct rapid prototyping and incremental development at the same time. That's a sure way to lose the cohesion of your development team!

Managing OO Development

Perhaps OO development is more challenging to manage, but there are significant advantages. OO development can give managers a better understanding of software systems without having to be programmers, allowing them to make better strategic decisions at critical points during development. The OO life cycle, as described above, is extremely flexible, allowing opportunity for creative management. For example, OO development is particularly well suited for phased development, is adaptable to changing markets, and may even allow parallel product development for slightly different markets.

Unfortunately, if left uncontrolled, these strategies can also produce chaos, unsettling both managers and developers. Questions arise such as, when do you move to the next stage, when do you know you are done, and isn't there a danger of endless iteration?

Incremental development dictates that the problem be divided into chunks. Therefore, it helps to view each application or product as a series of releases offering additional functionality with each version. This means separating the list of requirements into basic functionality and manageable chunks of additional functionality. This should be done even if most of the interim "versions" are incomplete and could never actually be released or deployed. The subrequirements are then given as the input to each iteration cycle and define the scope of that cycle. Not to say that other functionality can not be discussed, but a smaller list of requirements focuses the discussion and output of meetings for that cycle. No more meetings where participants leave more confused and overwhelmed than before.

Note that the subrequirements you select should make sense from the perspective of both the developer and customer. Customers may be involved in negotiating the next set of requirements so that the results of each iteration meet their expectations.

The "fuzzy line" between analysis and design can be avoided by using appropriate methods and notations at each stage, clearly documenting the outputs and inputs. The next section addresses selecting a method and notation.

It is natural for different people to work on different stages of development. Analysis is best conducted by a collection of domain experts, human factors specialists, and skilled OO designers. Design is best conducted by a collection of the same OO designers with additional programmers. If the output of each stage is well documented and easily interpreted, concurrent-staged development is also possible.

For example, OMG recommends that each cycle not exceed 90 days (see *Object Analysis and Design, Volume 1: Reference Model*). Using this as a benchmark, one approach is to simply schedule stages in succession, one month each for analysis, design and implementation. However, this is probably not the best use of time and resources (for example, human factors specialists would have a two month gap between cycles). Another approach is to release the management control slightly and allow the problem to dictate the scheduling of stages. This will lead to *concurrent-staged development* where analysis, design, and implementation appear to take place simultaneously.

Actually, this approach is not as anarchistic as it appears. There is a natural tendency to stagger stages within a cycle and then progressively shift emphasis from analysis to design in the second quarter and from design to implementation in the third. Realistically, some designers will participate in both analysis and design, and some programmers will participate in both design and implementation. Taking this into account, cycles can be staggered to the extent that team members are not overworked.

An example of concurrent-staged development is illustrated in Figure 3–3, where the duration of each cycle is three months (time increases horizontally). The level of effort in the first month primarily focuses on analysis. In the second month of a cycle, focus shifts to design, freeing up the analysis staff to begin on the next cycle. Similarly, in the third month, focus shifts to implementation, freeing the design staff to begin on the next cycle. At the same time, the level of effort on analysis of the second cycle peaks. By staggering cycles in this way, four cycles are completed in nine months instead of twelve.

Figure 3–3   Example of concurrent-staged development.

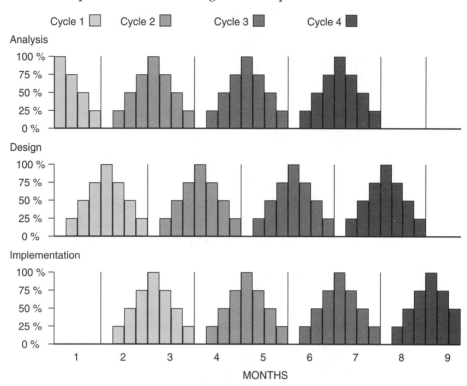

In reality you'll find that analysts and programmers that do not participate directly in design have periodic slack time while designers do most of the work. This is actually good because OO development requires more emphasis on design, and the output of design translates directly into the implementation. In fact, designers/programmers are often the core team members, whereas analysts and junior programmers offer services that can be shared between projects.

Any slack time programmers have can be easily filled by documenting the code and writing those needed class specifications. Human factors specialists (part of the analysis team) can begin drafting the user manuals. Try to recruit versatile team members—not stereotypes. Documentation is so important for knowledge transfer to QA and promoting enterprise-wide reuse, that it should be considered a normal on-going activity, not delayed until the end of the project.

The fear of endless iteration is really unfounded. The prototype may be evaluated at the end of each cycle, called *checkpointing*, at which time management may elect to re-focus the project, change the project organization and/or change the management structure accordingly. The system is "done" when it meets *all* the original requirements or exhausts all the time and resources. Not intending to be facetious, but exhausting time and resources is sometimes a reasonable way to operate a project. Customers can be intimately involved in the checkpointing process and get exactly what they pay for at every step of the way. After all, customer satisfaction is the only true measure of success.

Selecting a Method

Structured design techniques, such as data flow diagrams, do not translate well into an object model, so don't try using these methods with OO technology. Instead, select an appropriate OO analysis and design method that suits your application, style of development, and implementation environment.

A *method* is a guide that outlines the steps of analysis and/or design and may in addition provide techniques, notations and/or OO CASE tools. As mentioned earlier, *Object Analysis and Design, Description of Methods* identifies over twenty different OO analysis and design methods to choose from including the Booch, Coad, Object Behavior Analysis (OBA), OOSE by Jacobson, OMT by Rumbaugh, and Shlaer/Mellor methods. A comparison of all these methods is beyond the scope of this book, see *Object Analysis and Design, Comparison of Methods* by Andrew Hutt.

However, when evaluating methods it is helpful to refer to Booch's categories of four different approaches to analysis (see *Object-Oriented Analysis and Design with Applications* by Booch).

❑   The *classic approach* is based on classical categorization, identifying objects with nouns such as people, places, or things, and methods with verbs.

❑   *Behavior analysis* describes the entire system in terms of behaviors, and identifies objects as the exhibitors and participants of this behavior. Objects are also grouped by behavior as opposed to common attributes.

❑   *Domain analysis* identifies the objects directly from interviews with domain experts and by examining existing systems used in the domain. The goal is to discover objects that can be used by multiple applications in the target domain.

❏ *Use case analysis* translates the requirements into a number of scenarios describing the user's interaction with the system. Analyzing these scenarios then reveals the objects.

Although not all methods fall into one of these categories, they may be similar to one or use a combination of these techniques. Whatever method you select for your organization will be the right one as long as it produces the desired results; it translates the functional description into an object model with associated behaviors.

Summary

The process of OO development is so significantly different from structured analysis, design, and programming, that it requires a modified life cycle, different management approach, and new methods and notations:

❏ The waterfall life cycle is too rigid. It does not allow changes which are inevitable.

❏ The OO life cycle does not significantly alter the stages of development but encourages iteration.

❏ Commonly used iteration strategies are rapid prototyping and incremental development.

❏ Managing OO development and these iteration strategies is more challenging but provides better control.

❏ Selecting a method and notation that fits your style of organization is as important as selecting the development environment.

Analysis

4

This chapter describes OO analysis and how it differs from "traditional" analysis. The Jacobson Method is used to develop an example application that will be featured throughout this book. The example application is an analysis tool; therefore, developing the requirements for this application is itself a lesson in OO analysis.

What Is OO Analysis?

The goal of analysis is to obtain a complete understanding of the problem domain, and provide a good foundation for design. In addition, OO analysis begins to translate the functional description of the system into objects and their behaviors.

The input to OO analysis depends on how well defined the problem is but may include any or all of the following: a problem statement, detailed requirements specification, and dialogue with domain experts. The requirements specification, typically a textual document enumerating the desired system features, may contain implementation constraints. The true requirements are independent of any implementation, and therefore, must be extracted from this document. If there is no requirements specification or it is incomplete, a large portion of this activity will be dedicated to discovering and documenting the user requirements.

The outputs of OO analysis are the high-level objects for the system and their relationships, and a description of the system behaviors in terms of these objects. Ideally, this is understandable by all (users, managers, and developers alike), and establishes the terminology used throughout the project.

How the results of OO analysis are documented is important to the success of the project; it is the glue between the requirements and the design and the basis for high-level discussions between different parties. It can even be considered the contract between the client and developers. Analysis requires human interaction and you can't afford to be misunderstood at this early stage of development.

An on-line document or OO CASE tool that supports browsing is ideal to view the analysis since all team members need equal access to the evolving object model, including new team members, non-programmers (that is, managers and domain experts), and other team members, such as technical writers, not participating directly in analysis. Also, individuals participating in high-level strategic modelling need access to object models developed by multiple projects to help them in the task of identifying enterprise-wide reusable components and designs.

You may be confused about how analysis differs from design—where analysis ends and design begins. As stated earlier, the advantage of OO systems is that a common object model is developed throughout the life cycle and thus there is less chance of misinterpretation from one stage to the next. However, without a clear understanding of the process and some guidelines, stages of the OO life cycle can become muddled, producing poor results. Using appropriate methods, notations, and tools at each stage of development helps to distinguish the input and output from each. The method you select should also suit your application and style of development.

The Jacobson Method

Object-Oriented Software Engineering (OOSE) or simply the *Jacobson Method* is a complete life cycle method developed over the past twenty years. In this book, the Jacobson Method specifically refers to the method described in *Object-Oriented Software Engineering* by Ivar Jacobson and colleagues. *Objectory* is the corresponding OO CASE tool now supplied by Rational, not a method. This book only covers the analysis and design portions of the Jacobson Method.

The Jacobson Method conducts use case analysis to discover the principal objects, classes, and their attributes. Use case analysis translates requirements into a number of use cases describing the user's interaction with the system. These use cases reveal some of the objects, and are the basis for exploring object interactions. The use cases can even be used to test the final system and help write the user manual. Use case analysis is very effective in developing "user friendly" systems, because objects are discovered by modeling system behaviors from the user's perspective, not the computer's.

The Jacobson Method also makes a clear distinction between analysis and design. Analysis should produce a logical model not restricted by the implementation environment, since it's the implementation environment that most often changes. In this way, most changes affect only the design model and implementation. This is better in tune with the OO philosophy, to allow change but limit the impact. The Jacobson Method uses different notations during analysis and design to emphasize the difference.

Specifically, the Jacobson Method divides the process of software development into three stages: Analysis, Construction, and Testing. The method that applies to the analysis stage is covered in this chapter. The construction stage, equivalent to OMG's design modelling, implementation modelling, and construction stages, is covered in Chapter 5—*Design*.

The inputs to the Jacobson Method are the requirements specification and customer interviews, and the outputs are a *requirements model* and an *analysis model* described below.

The Requirements Model

The purpose of the *requirements model* is to document all the functional requirements of the system from the user's perspective, and consists of use cases, interface descriptions, and (optionally) a domain object model and glossary. *Use cases* describe the user's interaction with the system, and *interface descriptions* are snapshots of what the user interface might look like. The *domain object model* consists of objects that have a direct counterpart in the problem domain, often easily derived from the use cases. The *glossary* is used to list all terms or reserved words discovered during analysis.

The steps in developing the requirements model are: (1) identify the types of users or roles that user's play, called *actors*; (2) enumerate the use cases that cover the required functionality by examining the tasks each actor performs; (3) document use cases annotating each with interface descriptions (for example, screen snapshots); (4) extract the domain objects from the use cases; and (5) refine the requirements model by identifying "abstract use cases." A sixth step, (6) reenact the use cases, to close the loop is borrowed from *Objects—Born and Bred* by Elizabeth Gibson.

The Jacobson Method recommends identifying the implementation environment (a step that is part of the design stage) be done in parallel with the analysis steps listed above (this is an example of concurrent-staged development as described in Chapter 3—*The Process*). This approach helps sort out the items listed in the requirements specification that are implementation dependent.

This whole process is iterative and incremental, as described in Chapter 3, and can be combined with rapid prototyping (for example, use Open-Step's Graphical User Interface (GUI) builder, Interface Builder, to create a mock system).

The Analysis Model

Once the requirements model is fairly complete, create the analysis model. *Robustness analysis* is the process of creating the *analysis model*, an elaboration of the domain object model but still independent of the implementation environment. The premise is that it is the implementation environment that most often changes, and therefore it should be clearly documented which part of the design is implementation independent. The goal is to design more maintainable and extensible systems. To insure this step is not forgotten, the Jacobson Method makes robustness analysis a formal step of the analysis stage. Other methods proceed directly to design from just the domain object model.[†]

To lessen the impact of change on the analysis model and consequently the entire system, the Jacobson Method uses a paradigm similar to the Model-View-Controller (MVC) paradigm in Smalltalk. Objects in the analysis model are either *entity objects* that model persistent information, *interface objects* that implement the interface, or *control objects* that encapsulate functionality that operates on several entity objects and returns results to interface objects. Thus, developing this analysis model

---

† Note, the design modelling stage as defined by OMG is not equivalent to robustness analysis, since the design of external specification may still be dependent on the implementation environment.

requires distributing the behavior specified in the use cases among these three types of objects and documenting the responsibilities of each.

In Smalltalk, the *MVC paradigm* is a user interface strategy for allowing multiple views of the same model. However, the Jacobson Method definition is more abstract, where interface objects may also interface with other information systems (not just users), and control objects are more general purpose. Therefore, the Jacobson Method triad is really a generalization of Smalltalk's MVC paradigm.

The Application Kit is a collection of OpenStep classes used to construct GUIs. The most commonly used class is NSView and its subclasses, similar in concept to a Smalltalk view. To be consistent with OpenStep documentation, the term *view* will hereafter refer to a specific type of interface object, a descendent of NSView.

In general, there are two types of control objects: those that are tightly coupled to a specific entity and interface object, and those that are shared by many different types of objects (for example, in the implementation of some mechanism). You may elect not to use control objects in your design, in which case the control object behavior is just distributed between the interface and entity object. Control objects help isolate change, however, producing more reusable and extensible systems (which is very important for large enterprises) as explained in *Object Analysis and Design, Description of Methods*, edited by Andrew Hutt:

> *Separating out more specific functionality into control objects results in more generalized behaviors in entity objects. The entity objects thus hold functionality that is more reusable across various or new use cases, and the control objects encapsulate interrelated functionality that might otherwise be scattered.*

Example: Cards Application

This example application, called *Cards*, is a computerized implementation of CRC cards as described by Kent Beck and Ward Cunningham in *A Laboratory for Teaching Object-Oriented Thinking*. CRC cards are used by a variety of OO analysis methods, therefore the Cards application is not only a good example but a useful tool (the finished application is included on the enclosed disk). In this example, you'll use CRC cards to document the domain objects.

Class, Responsibility, and Collaboration (CRC) cards are index cards used during analysis. Each card contains the object name, responsibilities of the object, and a list of collaborating objects. The *object name* establishes a vocabulary for discussing a design (although the distinction between classes and instances may be blurred). *Responsibilities* identify problems to be solved. *Collaborators* will send or be sent messages in the course of satisfying an object's responsibilities. Note, collaboration is not necessarily a symmetric relationship.

There is an implicit dependency between objects and their collaborators. A computerized implementation is further complicated by multiple users creating, editing, and sharing CRC cards (linking them together).

The actual implementation of Cards is non-trivial; it has aspects of both hypermedia (there is an implicit dependency between objects and their collaborators) and groupware (users create, edit and share CRC cards). In fact, Beck and Cunningham originally implemented CRC cards as a HyperCard stack on the Macintosh, but found paper index cards to be much more effective. Individuals seem to identify more with the objects and therefore understand them better by physically manipulating their corresponding index cards in meetings.

This physical interaction can't be replicated using the computer, but nevertheless there is a great need for this application. At some point the results of analysis need to be recorded and made available to others. Also, team members may not always be able to meet face to face, and with technology like Distributed Objects, real telecommuting is not far away. In any case, computerizing CRC cards is a challenging problem, ideal for illustrating the power of OpenStep, and therefore, is the theme application developed throughout this book.

Remember, analysis is really a people process, iterative by nature with multiple entry points, and difficult to describe in a linear format. Therefore, use this chapter as a guide and compare the results of this example to the analysis of your applications.

Problem Statement

Imagine you are contracted to develop an analysis tool and are given the following problem statement:

Problem Statement

Develop a computerized implementation of CRC cards to aid software development during the OO analysis stage. The tool will be used during meetings as well as off-line by one or two individuals. The tool must run on OpenStep and integrate with other OpenStep development tools. Refer to the original OOPSLA paper that describes CRC cards and their usage.

Since there is no requirements specification, the first step is to compile a list of system responsibilities extracted from the OOPSLA paper and interviews with users.

The Beck and Cunningham paper, reprinted in Appendix A—*A Laboratory For Teaching OO Thinking*, is extremely informative because it not only describes the process of using CRC cards, but contains experiences from using the index cards in a course called "Thinking with Objects." In essence, Beck and Cunningham have already conducted user studies with index cards as the prototype for the computerized CRC cards. So, first extract definitions and initial "system responsibilities" from this paper.

System Responsibilities

❑   Cards should be the size of 4 X 6 inch index cards containing the object or class name, a list of responsibilities, and list of collaborators as in:

> **Name: Agent**
>
> **Responsibilities:** Enter textual description of the agent's responsibilities or behaviors here.
>
> **Collaborators:** List collaborators here.

❑   Quickly add, delete, and copy cards.

❑   Save and load cards.

❑   Support working in teams.

❑   Quickly organize and spatially address cards.

❑   Highlight cards while executing a scenario.

❑   Maintain the context established by moving and discussing cards.

Examples of common card organizations:

❑   Overlapping cards may imply close collaboration.

❑   Cards placed above may imply supervision.

❑   A card representing "part of" another object is often arranged below that card hierarchically.

❑   Refinements of an abstraction may be collected and handled as a single pile of cards with the most abstract card on top representing the rest.

Next, interview the users of the Cards application to verify the list above and add more system responsibilities. As Gibson advises, it's important not to make assumptions and not to ask leading questions; let users express in their own words the problems with the current system. Here is an example of interview results with fictitious users.

Report on Interviews with Users

The users specifically request a computerization of the CRC cards to document the output of analysis meetings, aid in the presentation of cards during meetings (called walkthroughs), and support remote collaboration. Previous experience with CRC cards implemented using a word processor raised some specific concerns.

During analysis meetings, the computer display will be projected on a large screen, the computer keyboard will have a long cord so that it can be shared by passing it around the conference table, and an air mouse will be used so that the mouse can easily be shared to aid presentations.

In between analysis meetings, individuals will refine cards, continue analysis in small teams, and prepare card walkthroughs for the next meeting. At anytime individuals may browse through the database of cards to examine the object model as it evolves. Browsing must be easy so that all team members continue to use the tool so the model stays current.

Since the organization is very large, with facilities around the world, sometimes team members need to collaborate remotely. For example, marketing and support engineers closest to the real customers are not always located at the same physical site as system developers.

In an earlier project, a word processor with hyperlinks was used to implement CRC cards. The word processor could not keep up with the fast pace of analysis, and analysts began to spend more time maintaining the document than analyzing the problem. The hyperlinks were difficult to set up; only a few individuals mastered it and then became the sole editors of the document. Since the hyperlink implementation was textual and not object based, changing the name of an object broke all links to that object. Since changing names is very common when refining a design, the document quickly became out of date and no longer of any use.

Another problem was contention for the document itself. Only one person could edit the document at a time, and the document was in high demand for both editing and viewing. The computerized cards were supposed to be accessible by all team members. Unfortunately, because of these difficulties, the cards were only used during analysis meetings, and maintained by a few overworked individuals.

After studying this report more system responsibilities are added to the list:

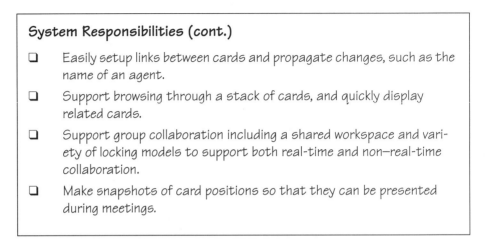

Before continuing, divide the system responsibilities into reasonable increments. It is already apparent that there are several blocks of functionality to be considered. The first block is the basic functionality to create, store, and update CRC cards. The second block is a more sophisticated recording of the user's spatial organization of cards, an assisting in walkthroughs, perhaps a supporting of other types of relationships such as part-whole or general to specific, and an automating of their spatial organizations. The third block is the support for group collaboration and shared database.

This is a good division of the requirements because the basic functionality is autonomous. Implementing the basic functionality will at least produce a demonstrable system. The second and third blocks can be implemented in either order, or in parallel if the resources are available. In any case, once the basic functionality is implemented, the management has the opportunity to reassess project goals and apply checkpointing strategies (for example, rubber-stamp or risk-driven using Boehm's Spiral Model described in the OMG document *Object Analysis and Design, Volume 1: Reference Model*).

This example focuses only on the basic system responsibilities in the first iteration and group collaboration in the second iteration:

First Iteration: Basic Functionality

The input to this iteration is simply this list of system responsibilities:

Basic Responsibilities

❑ Quickly add, delete, and copy cards.

❑ Accelerate repetitive actions such as creating a card followed by editing the agent's name and responsibilities field.

❑ Support creating cards in rapid succession with minimal key and mouse strokes.

❑ Easily set up links between cards and propagate changes, such as the name of an agent.

❑ Support browsing through a stack of cards and quickly display related cards.

❑ Save and load cards.

Step 1:   Identify the actors, the types of users or roles that users play.

This is the first step in developing the use cases portion of the requirements model.

In this example, all software project team members should have access to the cards database. The team members include managers, human factors specialists, domain experts, analysts, designers, programmers, and even technical writers. However, each type of user interacts with the system in the same way, so there is really only one actor, the "user." If there were other users who use the system differently, as in a "system administrator," then they would be other actors because the roles are very different.

Step 2:   Enumerate the use cases that cover the required functionality by examining the tasks each actor performs.

All team members need the ability to browse and search for cards. However, only individuals participating directly in analysis need to create cards. So, first examine the tasks that analysts perform since tasks performed by other actors will probably be a subset of these.

Analysts will use some OO Analysis method which conveniently provides a structure for discovering use cases. For example, analysts will routinely perform these actions:

1.   Start the application and load cards from disk (if they exist).

2.   Create a card for each agent, give each agent a name, and enumerate its responsibilities.

3.   Identify the relationships between agents and add the corresponding collaborators to each card.

4.   Browse through the cards.

5.   Refine the design by changing the names of agents or splitting them into two agents, deleting cards, adding and removing collaborators, and updating the responsibilities.

6.   Save the cards on disk.

7.   Quit the application.

8.   Continue the above steps until the analysis is complete.

From this derive the primary use cases:

❏   Creating cards.

❏   Browsing cards.

❏   Editing cards.

❏   Saving and loading cards.

All other actors have read-only permissions so their tasks include just loading and browsing cards. The actions of opening cards and opening collaborator cards are really secondary use cases—they support the *Browsing cards* primary use case.

The rest of this section will focus on these use cases: *Creating cards, Browsing cards* and *Editing cards*.

Step 3:   Document use cases annotating each with interface descriptions.

Each use case consists of a narrative description of the steps interlaced with snapshots of the user interface. Be careful not to include implementation details in the text, and always use active voice so that it's clear who initiates actions. You may also emphasize the initial objects and attributes in the descriptive text (for example, underline them). The snapshots are just sketches of what the user interface might look like to aid in understanding use cases, and are therefore optional.

If the user interface is not too complicated, Interface Builder can be used to create these snapshots. Interface Builder can also be used to play back snapshots in sequence (create each snapshot in a window, and open them in succession), or simply used to create figures for your documents.

The most common course of action is documented first, simplifying subsequent use cases. The first use case, *Creating cards*, describes the process of creating CRC cards, and uses Interface Builder snapshots as illustrations.

Use Case 1: Creating Cards

(1)   The user creates a card for each agent.

(2)   The user enters the agent's name and description of its responsibilities.

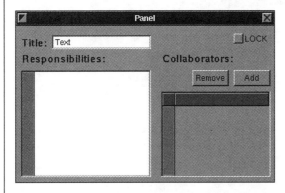

(3)   The user then identifies the relationships between agents and adds the corresponding collaborators to each card.

The second use case, *Browsing cards*, describes in more detail how the user navigates.

Use Case 2: Browsing Cards

(1)   The user launches the program and an index appears listing all the cards.

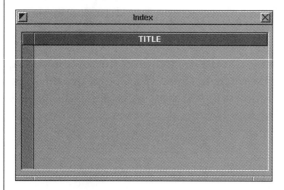

(2)   The user opens a card by selecting it from the index, and that card appears.

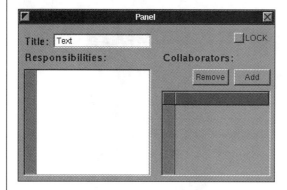

(3)   The user opens a collaborator's card by selecting it from the collaborators list, and that card appears.

The third use case, *Editing cards*, does not repeat steps covered in other use cases; it references them instead. This use case actually documents multiple scenarios (steps 2-4 are optional paths) and also reveals several new secondary use cases such as *Deleting cards*.

Use Case 3: Editing Cards

(1)   The user opens the card that needs to be changed (see *Browsing cards*).

(2)   The user optionally changes the name of the agent (this will propagate the change to the index and all other cards that reference this agent).

(3)   The user optionally edits the responsibilities text.

(4)   The user optionally adds and removes collaborators.

(5)   The user deletes obsolete cards (this will remove the deleted card from the index and all other cards that list it as a collaborator).

(6)   Steps 1-5 are repeated until the user is done.

Step 4:   Extract the domain objects from the use cases.

Discover the domain objects by determining who or what is responsible for the behaviors documented in the use cases above. Note that most of these objects will correspond to objects in the design. Also, during analysis it's okay to blur the distinction between classes and instances (the distinction will be made later during design). You can use OO notation (for example, the notation presented by Jacobson) or, as in this example, use CRC cards to document the domain object model. CRC cards can also function as a glossary because there's a card for each potential object and the descriptions contain other project terms.

Finding the objects and their properties is straightforward. There is an *agent* that has the properties of a *name*, a *textual description of its responsibilities* and a *list of collaborators*, other agents. The agent is represented by a *card* that allows the user to view and change its attributes. There are many agents and only one *index* that contains *a list of all the agents* (represented by another user interface object yet to be determined).

Therefore the initial objects are Agent, Index and Card whose properties and behaviors are documented using CRC cards illustrated in Figure 4–1.

Figure 4–1   Example CRC cards.

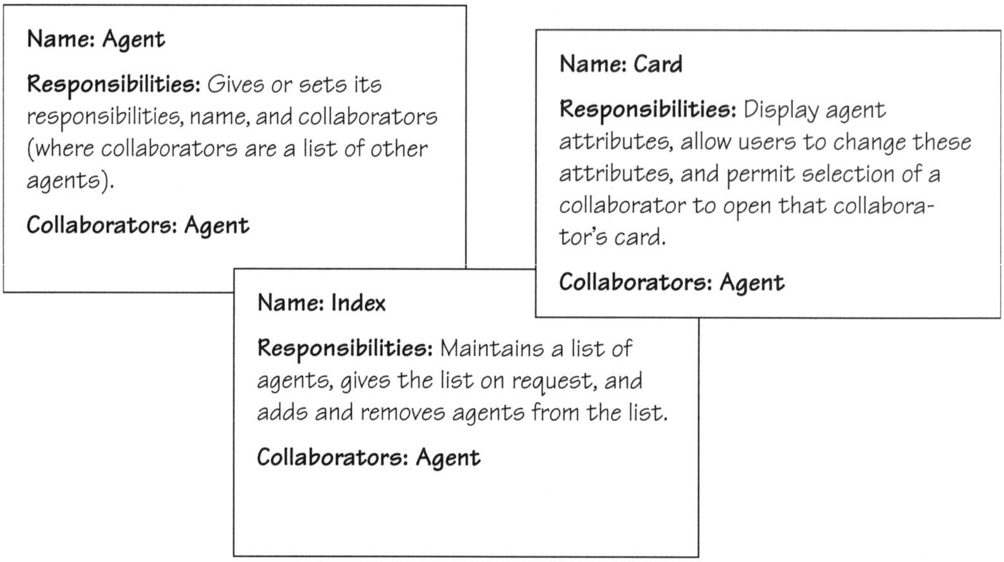

```
┌─────────────────────────────────────┐
│ Name: Agent                          │
│                                      │
│ Responsibilities: Gives or sets its  │
│ responsibilities, name, and collaborators
│ (where collaborators are a list of other
│ agents).                             │
│                                      │
│ Collaborators: Agent                 │
└──────────────────┬───────────────────┘
                   │
```

```
┌──────────────────────────────────────┐
│ Name: Card                             │
│                                        │
│ Responsibilities: Display agent        │
│ attributes, allow users to change these│
│ attributes, and permit selection of a  │
│ collaborator to open that collabora-   │
│ tor's card.                            │
│                                        │
│ Collaborators: Agent                   │
└────────────────────────────────────────┘
```

```
┌──────────────────────────────────────┐
│ Name: Index                            │
│                                        │
│ Responsibilities: Maintains a list of  │
│ agents, gives the list on request, and │
│ adds and removes agents from the list. │
│                                        │
│ Collaborators: Agent                   │
└────────────────────────────────────────┘
```

Step 5:   Refine the requirements model by identifying "abstract use cases."

In this step you analyze the use cases and extract commonality by creating new use cases, called *abstract use cases*. This step should be done after all the concrete use cases are documented.

In this example, there are no obvious abstract use cases.

Step 6:   Reenact the use cases.

Walk through the use cases to verify that the objects discovered so far are sufficient. This step can be as informal or formal as you like. Beck and Cunningham suggest an informal approach:

> *We encourage learners to pick up the card whose role they are assuming while "executing" a scenario. It is not unusual to see a designer with a card in each hand, waving them about, making a strong identification with the objects while describing their collaboration.*

Whatever approach you use, it is important to notice any behaviors not covered by the existing objects. For example, when changing the name or deleting an agent, cards are magically updated. Remember, agents have a list of collaborating agents, but this is not necessarily a symmetric relationship. Therefore, agents have no way of knowing which other agents collaborate with them, and can't notify them if their name changes or they are deleted. Something is missing that needs to keep track of these object "links." Without stating how the linking is implemented, add a CRC card for an object, called *LinkManager*, as a place holder for this behavior to be refined during design (see Figure 4–2).

Figure 4–2   LinkManager CRC card.

```
Name: LinkManager

Responsibilities: Keeps track of the
links between all objects. Given any
object, will return all objects linked to it
and vice versa.

Collaborators: all objects
```

In general, this step need not be rigorous since it will be repeated later during the design stage using interaction diagrams. In fact, the Jacobson Method derives the interaction diagrams directly from the use cases. The goal of this step is simply to find the obvious flaws in the domain object model.

Step 7:   Robustness analysis

At this point a requirements model exists consisting of use cases, screen snapshots, and domain objects. Now you divide or classify the domain objects as entity, control, and interface objects.

In this example, Agent, Author, and Index are clearly entity objects since they must survive beyond the execution of this program and will probably be stored in a database that multiple users can access. On the other hand, Card is an interface object that displays an Agent to the user. Link-Manager is an example of a control object that provides links between any object.

Next, draw diagrams illustrating the relationships between these objects using the Jacobson Method analysis model notation. The notation consists of a symbol for each object type (see Figure 4–3) and directed lines between the symbols to designate object associations. Directed lines can either be labeled with a verb phrase such as "depends on" designating the type of association, or a noun designating the *part* of a part-whole relationship. Cardinality can be appended to the label such as [1] indicating a one-to-one or [1..N] indicating a one-to-many relationship, where all associations are uni-directional.

Figure 4–3   Object type symbols.

By reviewing the CRC cards in Figure 4–1, identify the associations between the objects and create the diagram in Figure 4–4. An Index has many *agents* which are instances of Agent. An Agent has many *collaborators* which are instances of Agent, and many interface objects (to support group collaboration) which are instances of Card (whereas a Card has only one entity object which is an instance of Agent). Note, the labels *agents*, *collaborators*, and *model* will most likely become instance variables in the corresponding classes.

Figure 4–4   Index-Agent-Card association diagram.

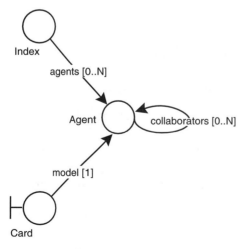

It may help to document some of the interface object details as well, especially if your user interface is complicated and not easily prototyped using Interface Builder. For example, Figure 4–5 illustrates the associations between Card and its parts. However, since the Cards interface is actually very simply, you would never specify this level of detail during analysis. These decisions are better delayed until design.

Figure 4–5   Card association diagram.

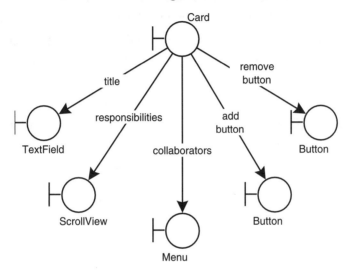

Second Iteration: Group Collaboration

The remaining chunks of system responsibilities are support for the user's spatial organization of cards and group collaboration. Group collaboration will be addressed next since it is an ideal opportunity to demonstrate the power of Distributed Objects.

The following subset of system responsibilities is the input to this iteration:

Group Collaboration System Responsibilities

❏   Support group collaboration including a shared workspace and variety of locking models to support both real time and non-real time collaboration.

Step 1:   Identify the actors, the types of users or roles that users play.

There are no new actors specifically for group collaboration. All actors discovered in the first iteration will have the ability to collaborate with other users. The only difference is that some will have read-only permissions and others have read/write permissions.

Step 2:   Enumerate the use cases that cover the required functionality by examining the tasks each actor performs.

The primary use case for group collaboration should describe how users create and join a virtual meeting. It should also describe how users lock cards for editing. This use case is simply called *Group collaboration*.

Step 3:   Document use cases annotating each with interface descriptions.

The *Group collaboration* use case need not be as descriptive as earlier use cases, documented in the first iteration. *Creating cards*, *Editing cards*, and *Browsing cards* are secondary use cases—they support the *Group collaboration* use case.

Use Case 4: Group Collaboration

(1)   A user opens a session, selects a level of concurrency (strict locking or free form), and advertises the new session to others.

(2)   Users can see who is connected to the session in real time.

(3)   Each user can create cards and add them to the shared workspace (see *Creating Cards*). All cards, independent of the authors, appear in every user's index.

(4)   Users can view cards (see *Browsing Cards*) and edit cards (see *Editing Cards*) created by other users. Cards created by one user can have collaborators created by another user.

(5)   If using strict locking, users must lock cards before editing them. If using free form, users may edit cards concurrently. In this case, cards or fields of cards are implicitly locked before the user begins editing them.

(6)   Users may steal locks away from other users if they are idle too long (for example, someone stepped out to lunch).

(7)   Users can view additional information about each card, such as the author, date last modified, version number, and state (for example, displayed in the index).

(8)   Users can join and leave a session at any time by quitting their application. Leaving a session will implicitly release cards locked by the user.

(9)   Steps 2–8 are repeated in any sequence until the session (the virtual meeting) is concluded.

Step 4:   Extract the domain objects from the use cases.

In this example, the shared workspace will contain all the entity objects: instances of Agent, and Index. Although each user interacts with his or her own instance of an index interface object, there is only one index entity object shared by all users. Since the index maintains the list of all agents, it is essentially the root object of this shared workspace (all agents are *part of* the index). Other objects that must be shared are the properties of the session itself (such as the locking mode and the participants).

Existing objects need to be refined, such as Agent (add the properties: author, date, and lock state), and some new objects need to be created to handle the shared session information (for example, objects Author and Session with locking mode properties). Figure 4–6 shows the updated and new CRC cards.

Figure 4–6   More example CRC cards.

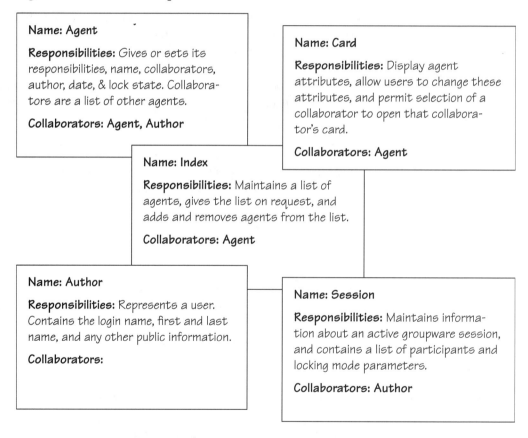

At this point you could either complete the rest of this iteration, or in true incremental, non-staged style of development, skip to design (Chapter 7—*Distributed Objects* continues this iteration by designing and implementing these groupware features).

Summary

This chapter describes the steps of OO analysis, how it differs from design, and applies methods and notations in the development of an example application called Cards.

OO analysis is the process of translating the functional description of the system into objects and their behaviors. The input to OO analysis is the same as traditional analysis: the problem statement, detailed requirements specification, and dialogue with domain experts. The outputs are the high-level objects, their relationships, and behaviors. Most important, OO analysis establishes the terminology used throughout the project.

A good method and notation helps to guide the process and distinguish the output of analysis from the output of design. The method used in this chapter, the Jacobson Method, advocates use case analysis which translates the requirements into use cases describing user interactions. Studying these use cases reveals the objects and their behaviors. The use cases can also be used to test the system and write user manuals. Most importantly, use case analysis is effective in developing user friendly systems because objects are discovered from the user's perspective—not the computer's.

The output of the Jacobson Method is the requirements model and analysis model. The *requirements model* consists of use cases, *interface descriptions* that can be created using OpenStep's GUI builder called Interface Builder, and a *domain object model* that may be documented using CRC cards.

The Jacobson Method adds an additional step called robustness analysis. *Robustness analysis* produces an *analysis model* that is an elaboration of the domain object model, but is still implementation environment independent. Robustness analysis distributes the behavior specified in the use cases among three types of objects: *entity objects* that model persistent information, *interface objects* that implement the interface, and *control objects* that encapsulate functionality that operates on several entity objects and returns results to interface objects.

Although control objects are less common in an OO design than entity and interface objects, when used they can be very effective in producing maintainable and extensible systems.

Design 5

This chapter explains how design differs from analysis and applies the Jacobson Method and Booch Notation to further develop the example Cards application started in Chapter 4—*Analysis*. Before presenting the design example, the design steps of the Jacobson Method are outlined and the Booch Notation is introduced.

What Is OO Design?

The process of OO design is fundamentally the same as OO analysis, but the emphasis shifts from *what* to *how*. With the Jacobson Method, the emphasis also shifts from implementation independence to implementation dependence, by refining the analysis models into a complete design, meeting all the computer imposed constraints of modularity, distribution, efficiency, and quality.

The input to OO design is naturally the output of OO analysis, high-level objects, their relationships, and behaviors. The output of OO design depends on the method used, but may include class specifications, class hierarchies, object part-whole relationships, message traces, groupings of classes into modules, and the architecture of the applications and processes. It is not necessary to document every detail, but certainly the most interesting aspects of the system should be captured.

An OO design method is recommended to help guide the design process, and the output is best captured using an appropriate OO design notation. At this level of development, an OO CASE tool that helps to maintain the relationships between diagrams, class specifications, and eventually source code is desirable, but a good drawing tool and word processor will suffice.

Other tools used during design are the frameworks that you either purchased, developed yourself, or acquired along the way (for example,

OpenStep). A *framework* is a collection of classes and mechanisms that provides a set of services for a particular domain, such as user interface or database.

A *mechanism* is a design that specifies how a collection of objects cooperate to provide some service. In Objective-C, mechanisms might consist of a couple of control objects offering some service and protocols for client objects that use this service. For example, the Application Kit, the OpenStep framework containing classes for Graphical User Interface (GUI) construction, provides a mechanism for dragging application images between windows. Application objects that conform to the NSDraggingSource protocol suddenly become draggable objects with very little programming effort. Thus, mechanisms are used to implement common behavior at a higher level of reuse than is possible with individual classes.

OpenStep provides many mechanisms that you can leverage in the implementation of your applications. For example, most objects use the initialization and deallocation mechanisms inherited from NSObject. These and other mechanisms, such as the autorelease and notification center mechanisms, will be used to implement the Cards application. Each mechanism will be described in detail the first time it's used.

The Jacobson Method

At this point in the development process, the requirements model (consisting of the use cases, interface descriptions, and domain objects) and the analysis model (classifying objects as entity, interface, and control objects) are fairly complete. These models are still independent of the implementation environment. Therefore, the goal of design is to produce a model that takes into account the implementation language, distributed environment, database, and any performance requirements. Also, the design model leverages the tools, frameworks, and mechanisms provided by the implementation environment.

The Jacobson Method steps of design are roughly: (1) identify the implementation environment; (2) refine the analysis model, adding implementation strategies to produce the design model; (3) refine the design model using the use cases produced from analysis; (4) develop complete interface specifications of each object; (5) refine class specifications using state transition graphs; and (6) structure and implement the objects.

The Jacobson Method purposely uses a different notation for design than for analysis so that there is a clear separation between these stages. The first design model is just a translation of the analysis model into the design notation. Also, the Jacobson Method uses interaction diagrams to model the *stimuli,* or message flow, between objects. These interaction diagrams are produced by stepping through the use cases, and text from the use cases are used to annotate the diagrams. Later, text from the interaction diagrams can be used to draft the first class specifications. In this way, the Jacobson Method is traceable, ideally supported by an OO CASE tool.

Don't worry, this book doesn't assume you have access to an OO CASE tool. Therefore, the Jacobson Method is used as a guide for design and is not strictly followed.

The Booch Notation

The Booch Notation is used in this book because it incorporates aspects of both the Jacobson Method and the Object Modeling Technique (OMT), by James Rumbaugh, because the notation is now in the public domain to support a standard representation of OO designs. The notation is also very complete, providing various levels of detail; well suited for hybrid OO languages like Objective-C. Because of this versatility, the Booch Notation can be used in combination with almost any method you choose.

This book uses *Booch Lite,* just the essentials with the addition of a few advanced features. Booch Lite consists of class and class category diagrams, object diagrams, interaction diagrams, state transition diagrams (not covered in this book), module diagrams, and process diagrams. Appendix C—*Booch Lite* contains a complete description of these diagrams with notes for Objective-C. If you are unfamiliar with the Booch Notation, read Appendix C before continuing. If you are already familiar with the Booch Notation, here is a summary of adaptations made in this book:

❏   The role adornment in class and object diagrams is used to denote a class or object that conforms to an Objective-C protocol or informal protocol.

❏   Since class hierarchies are fundamentally different from part-whole relationships, these relationships will not be combined in class diagrams. A simple line drawing of a directed tree will be used to depict class hierarchies.

State transition diagrams are not used in this book and hence step (5) of the Jacobson Method will be skipped. When programming with Open-Step, you usually don't need to go to this level of detail. Most objects in your application will either be instances of OpenStep objects or will inherit from them. Thus your application objects are usually simple—they have no complex state worth modelling.

Example: Cards Application

You use the output of analysis as the guide during design: the requirements and the analysis models. The use cases discovered during analysis are:

❏   *Use Case 1: Creating Cards.*
❏   *Use Case 2: Browsing Cards.*
❏   *Use Case 3: Editing Cards.*
❏   *Use Case 4: Group Collaboration.*

The domain objects are Index, Agent, Card, LinkManager, Author and Session, documented using CRC cards:

❏   Figure 4–1—*Example of CRC cards.*
❏   Figure 4–2—*LinkManager CRC card.*
❏   Figure 4–6—*More example CRC cards.*

The analysis model classifies objects as either entity, interface, or control objects. The entity objects are: Index, Agent, Author, and Session. Card is an interface object and LinkManager is a control object. The analysis model is documented in figures:

❏   Figure 4–4—*Index-Agent-Card association diagram.*
❏   Figure 4–5—*Card association diagram.*

Step 1:   Identify implementation environment.

Since this is a book on OpenStep, Objective-C is the implementation language and you will leverage frameworks and mechanisms provided by OpenStep. Distributed Objects are used to implement the groupware features, and are covered in Chapter 7—*Distributed Objects*.

Step 2:   Produce first design model.

Add implementation strategies to the analysis model to produce the first design model. First, translate the analysis model diagrams developed in Chapter 4—*Analysis* into design diagrams using the Booch Notation. Figure 5–1 shows the first class diagram featuring Index, Agent, and Card.

Figure 5–1   Initial Index-Agent class diagram.

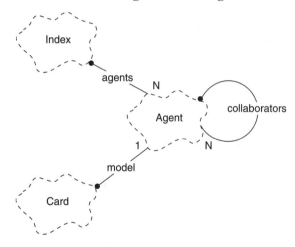

Since this is the design stage, you can use your implementation experience with OpenStep to improve the class diagram above. During analysis, Card was classified as an interface object. However, OpenStep already contains a complete set of interface objects that you will use to construct the user interface (with OpenStep's GUI builder, called Interface Builder). You will not need to create custom views by subclassing NSView.

At this point, you can use your OpenStep knowledge, specifically knowledge about how Interface Builder and the Application Kit works. There needs to be an object in this design that handles user actions (for example, when the user clicks a button). This object is typically the target in Interface Builder that will receiver action messages from interface objects (instances of NSView). This object is a classic control object that acts as an intermediary between the interface objects and the entity object. Because this object is a control object for Agent, call it *ControlAgent*. Similarly, there will be a control object for Index, called *ControlIndex*.

Figure 5–2 shows the updated class diagram (details of interface objects are left to the implementation). The associations between classes are labeled with the name of the instance variable that maintains that association. For example, ControlIndex and ControlAgent will have a **model** instance variable. If there is no label, the association is unspecified. The number on the target side of the association indicates the cardinality. For example, control objects have only one model, but Index and Agent maintain associations with many agents. Therefore, agents and collaborators are most likely container objects, instances of NSArray.

Figure 5–2   Index-Agent class diagram with control objects.

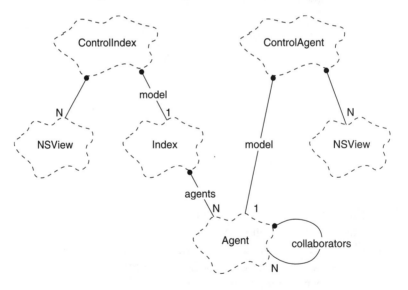

The analysis stage also produced a LinkManager control object for managing the links between cards. Luckily OpenStep provides us with a class, NSNotificationCenter, that has similar capabilities. NSNotificationCenter, or simply *the notification center*, implements a mechanism for broadcasting notifications from one object to many. Objects add themselves as observers of notifications specifying the notification name and/or source object (object that posts) and message to send. The sender then posts a notification to the center that broadcasts it to all interested objects. Notification names are just NSString objects that identify the type of notification and can be defined by your application.

The advantage of using the notification center is that the source objects that post notifications don't need to know anything about the receivers of notifications—these "links" between objects are managed by the notification center. This is ideal for encapsulating entity object implementations, like Agent, from control and interface object implementations. In this design, control objects know about entity objects, but entity objects know nothing about control or interface objects, thus making them more reusable enterprise wide.

Step 3:   Refine the design model using the use cases.

This example focuses on only the interesting aspects of the design. *Use Case 3: Editing Cards*, presented in Chapter 4—*Analysis*, poses interesting problems in synchronizing all the views. For example, Agent and Index views need to be updated if an agent's name changes and notified if an agent is deleted.

In this design, any object that "depends on" another will add itself as an observer of notifications posted by that object. Also, any object that "notifies dependents" will post a notification to the notification center. Specifically, an agent will post notifications of changes to itself, and add itself as an observer of change notifications posted by its collaborators. Index will also post change notifications and add itself as an observer of change notifications posted by all other agents. The types of notifications posted will be discovered using the use cases.

There are three user actions that need to be modeled from *Use Case 3: Editing Cards*: (1) changing the name of an agent, (2) adding and removing collaborators, and (3) deleting an agent. First, you need to define some notification names that agents will post:

```
AgentDidChangeTitleNotification
AgentDidChangeResponsibilitiesNotification
AgentDidAddCollaboratorsNotification
AgentDidRemoveCollaboratorsNotification
ObjectWillDeleteNotification
```

The next step is to trace the message flow of notifications using object and interaction diagrams. Model the first user action, changing the name of an agent, using an object diagram. In this and following examples, assume there is one instance of Index, **theIndex**, and two agents called **agent1** and **agent2** where **agent1** is a collaborator of **agent2**. Also, **theIndex**, **agent1**, and **agent2** each have corresponding control objects. Also, assume that the control objects have previously added themselves as observers of AgentDidChangeTitleNotifications posted by **agent1** and specified **agentDidChangeTitle:** as the callback selector.

The resulting object diagram is illustrated in Figure 5–3 where the message trace begins with sending **setTitle:** to **agent1** passing the new name as the argument. Agent's **setTitle:** changes the receiver's title and posts an AgentDidChangeTitleNotification. Consequently, the notification center sends **agentDidChangeTitle:** to each control object (order is actually non-deterministic), and the control objects update their corresponding views (interface objects not shown).

Figure 5–3   Object diagram for changing the name of an agent.

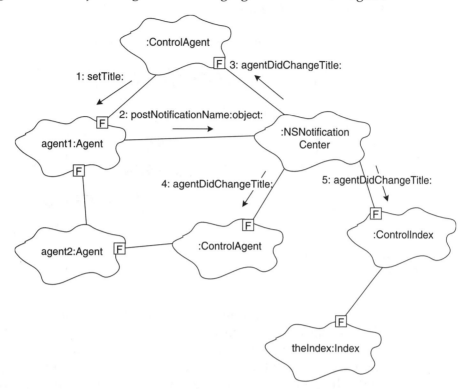

All selectors registered with the notification center (for example, **agent-DidChangeTitle:**) must take a single argument, an instance of NSNotification. NSNotification contains the name of the notification, the object that posted the notification and any additional user information (as an NSDictionary) that the receiver may use.

For example, ControlAgent's **agentDidChangeTitle:** method can get the object that posted the notification from the NSNotification object. If the returned object is its own model, then the view that displays its title is updated; otherwise the object is a collaborator and the view that displays the collaborators is updated.

Alternatively, an interaction diagram can be used to describe the message flow as in Figure 5–4. The interaction diagram is annotated with descriptive text describing the action of each message. The blocks are used to show the focus of control which is not obvious information when looking at an object diagram. If you are just modelling message flow, an interaction diagram is often more concise and easier to follow than an object diagram.

Figure 5–4   Interaction diagram for changing the name of an agent.

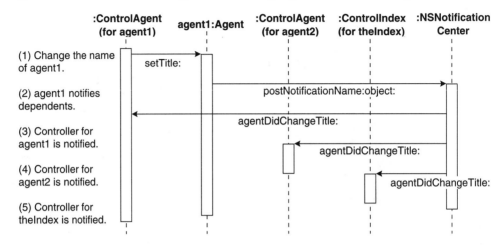

Note, the order of messages 3–5 in both diagrams is actually not known. The messages are synchronous, but NSNotificationCenter can not guarantee the order in which they are invoked. It's really a deficiency in both these diagrams not to show this information. You should append a note to the diagram whenever potential race conditions might occur.

The second user action, adding and removing collaborators, is less complicated since only an Agent's control object cares about changes to the list of collaborators. Adding and removing collaborators are similar actions, so only one case needs to be modelled. Figure 5–5 illustrates the message flow of adding a collaborator to an agent, where **agent1**'s control object previously added itself as an observer of AgentDidAddCollaboratorsNotifications posted by **agent1** and specified **agentDidAddCollaborators:** as the callback selector.

Figure 5–5   Object diagram for adding a collaborator.

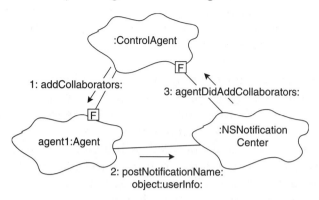

Note, the box containing the "F" is called a visibility adornment. The ControlAgent instance is a *field* of the notification center because the notification center maintains a reference to it once it became an observer of notifications (for example, perhaps its stored in a hash table). However, the visibility between **agent1** and the notification center is unspecified because the notification center is obtained elsewhere (you usually get the default notification center for your process from the NSNotification class).

In the case of adding a collaborator, **agent1** could pass the new collaborator in the **userInfo** argument when posting the notification. Instances of ControlAgent could then update the display more intelligently. These details will be delayed until the implementation stage.

The third user action, deleting an agent, is more complicated since not only do views need to be updated, but the agent needs to be removed from theIndex and any other agents that have it listed as a collaborator.

First you need to understand how OpenStep's release mechanism works. The *release mechanism* is designed to fix the "dangling reference" problem, a reference to a deallocated object. Each object has a reference count. Sending **retain** to an object increments the reference count and sending **release** decrements the reference count. An object is not actually deallocated until its reference count reaches zero. Therefore, by retaining objects you can insure that they are not inadvertently deallocated.

However, when the user deletes an agent in the Cards application, you really want that object to be deallocated, not simply decrease its reference count. Therefore, it's not enough to send **release** or **autorelease** to an Agent; other objects, such as its control object, retain it. (When using Distributed Objects, objects must retain objects they reference; see Chapter 7—*Distributed Objects*.) So you need to implement your own **delete** method, again leveraging the notification center.

The message flow for deleting an Agent is illustrated using an interaction diagram in Figure 5–6, where **agent1**, a collaborator of **agent2**, is deleted. Assume that the control objects for **agent1**, **agent2**, and **theIndex** have previously added themselves as observers of ObjectWillDeleteNotifications and specified **willDelete:** as the callback selector. The trace begins with **agent1**'s control object sending it **delete** (triggered by some user action). When notified, the control object for **agent1** releases itself and its views (not shown in diagram), but **theIndex** and **agent2** simply remove any references to **agent1** before it is deleted. **agent1** is deallocated when its reference count reaches zero.

Figure 5–6   Interaction diagram for deleting an agent.

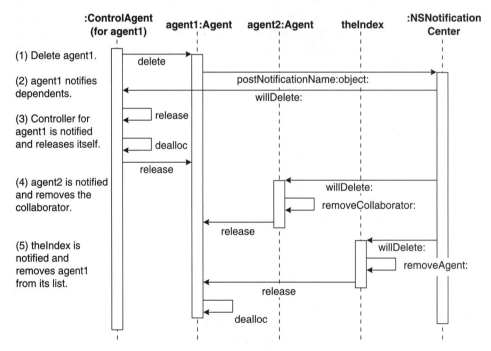

This interaction diagram is purposely simplified leaving out details such as the message flow resulting from sending **removeCollaborators:** to an Agent. This message flow is similar to that of sending **addCollaborators:** to an Agent shown in Figure 5–5, and therefore does not need to be repeated in this diagram. None of the interaction diagrams show the argument and return values of messages. The diagrams could be annotated to show this detail, but such details tend to clutter the diagram and are not really necessary—this is only the design stage, syntactical details can be left to the implementation.

Step 4:   Develop object interfaces.

Go through all the object and interaction diagrams and list the messages sent to each object. Capture the interface using the programming language (for example, create an Objective-C header file for each class) or using a class specification sheet. If using Jacobson style interaction diagrams the first description of each method can be taken from the margins.

For example, the messages sent to instances of Agent are:

- `setTitle:`
- `addCollaborators:`
- `removeCollaborators:`
- `delete`
- `willDelete`

From examining the object, interaction, and class diagrams, the initial Objective-C interface file for Agent can be derived as shown (Appendix D—*Class Specifications* contains complete class specifications for the finished Cards application):

```
@interface Agent : NSObject
{
    id collaborators;
    NSMutableString *responsibilities;
    NSMutableString *title;
}
- init;
- (void)dealloc;
- (void)addCollaborators:(id)anObject;
- (id)collaborators;
- (void)delete;
- (void)removeCollaborators:(id)anObject;
- (NSString *)responsibilities;
- (void)setResponsibilities:(NSString *)aString;
- (void)setTitle:(NSString *)aString;
- (NSString *)title;
- (void)willDelete:(NSNotification *)notification;
@end
```

Every entity class should have an **init** method to initialize instance variables and a **dealloc** method to release instance variables. The initialization and deallocation mechanisms are explained in detail in the next
chapter.

Similarly, the instance variables and methods for Index are derived from
the diagrams producing the following Objective-C interface file:

```
@interface Index : NSObject
{
    id agents;
}
- init;
- (void)dealloc;
- (void)addAgent:(id)anObject;
- (id)agents;
- (void)removeAgent:(id)anObject;
- (void)willDelete:(NSNotification *)notification;
@end
```

Step 5:   Refine object interfaces through state transition graphs.

This step can be skipped—most OpenStep applications don't have objects with complex states, and modelling state is arguably an implementation detail. For examples of this step, see *Object-Oriented Software Engineering* by Ivar Jacobson.

Step 6:   Structure and implement the objects.

So far, you have used every diagram except class hierarchies, class categories, module diagrams, and process diagrams. A *class category* is a logical grouping of related classes, whereas a *module* corresponds to a physical source file and a subsystem corresponds to a physical software library containing one or more class categories. The *process diagram* describes the physical relationship between devices and distribution of programs. Together these diagrams define the structure of the objects.

First you create the class hierarchy. In *Objects—Born and Bred*, Elizabeth Gibson points out that it is initially easier for people to classify objects in terms of state, not behavior. For example, people might readily group a real apple and wax apple in the same category because they look alike, but certainly they are very different since you can eat one and not the other. In an OO system, it is better to classify by behavior because the methods that ultimately implement this behavior are more valuable to inherit than the instance variables that represent state.

The Cards application is trivial where classification is concerned. Entity and control objects are all distinct and will therefore inherit from NSObject as shown in Figure 5–7.

Figure 5–7   Cards class hierarchy.

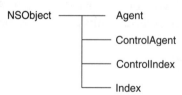

Furthermore, entity objects that model persistent information can be reused by multiple applications; therefore, they are separated into a different class category. The interface objects will be created using Interface Builder and are part of the Application Kit.

Figure 5–8 illustrates the class categories where *Models* and *Controllers* are the application class categories for entity and control objects respectively. Shaded icons are external to the design, part of OpenStep or other frameworks. Models is dependent, for example, on the Enterprise Objects Framework (EOF), and Controllers is dependent on Models and the Application Kit. All class categories are dependent on the Foundation Kit, an OpenStep framework containing all the basic classes. Both entity and control objects inherit from NSObject and use the notification center which belongs to the Foundation Kit.

Figure 5–8   Cards class category diagram.

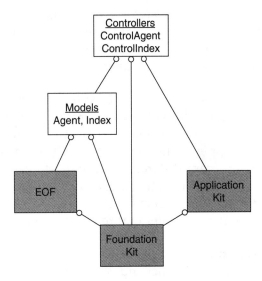

The module diagram in Figure 5–9 shows the relationships between subsystems. In this simplistic example, the Models class categories belongs to the *libmodel* subsystem, and the Controllers class category and nib files (containing views) belong to the Cards Application subsystem. (OpenStep and other external subsystems are not shown).

Figure 5–9   Cards module diagram.

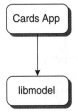

To complete this example, create a process diagram now, even though the groupware functionality will really be addressed later in Chapter 7. To support groupware, you can anticipate the need for a multi-user database server and a process that mediates between multiple Cards applications. Figure 5–10 illustrates a possible process diagram to support this functionality. The process diagram also needs to be accompanied by object diagrams showing the distributed object messaging to provide a complete picture of the interprocess communication. Distributed Objects will be addressed in Chapter 7.

Figure 5–10 Cards process diagram.

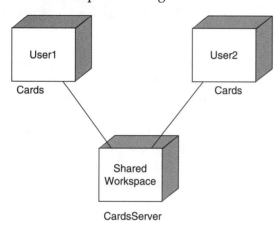

The implementation of Cards and introduction to OpenStep development tools is covered in Chapter 6.

Summary

During design, the emphasis shifts from *what* to *how* and from implementation independence to implementation dependence. The analysis model that was produced during the analysis stage is refined, meeting all the computer imposed constraints. The output of design includes class specifications and diagrams illustrating class hierarchies, part-whole relationships, message traces, groupings of classes into modules, and the architecture of devices and processes.

The design should leverage reusable components called *frameworks*, collections of classes and mechanisms that provide a set of services for a particular problem domain. *Mechanisms* are reusable designs that specify how a collection of objects cooperate to provide some service.

The specific steps in the Jacobson Method are: (1) identify the implementation environment; (2) refine the analysis model, adding implementation strategies and producing the design model; (3) refine the design model using the use cases; (4) develop complete interface specifications of each object; (5) refine class specifications using state transition graphs; and (6) structure and implement the objects.

The notation known as *Booch Lite* is used throughout this book with the exception of a few advanced features and adaptations for Objective-C (see Appendix C).

In general, class diagrams are used in step (2) and object diagrams and interaction diagrams are used in step (3). Interaction diagrams capture the message flow between objects by stepping through the use cases. Text from the use cases are used to annotate the diagrams and can be used to draft class specifications in step (4). Class hierarchy, class category, module, and process diagrams are used in step (6) to capture the structure of objects. Implementation of Cards is covered in Chapter 6—*Implementation*, and Chapter 7—*Distributed Objects*.

Implementation 6

This chapter covers the first iteration of the Cards implementation and is written in tutorial style—you may implement your own version of Cards while reading this chapter. This chapter assumes some familiarity with the window system but not with the developer tools. Therefore, actions such as creating a subclass using Interface Builder are covered in detail the first time they are mentioned. Step-by-step instructions for NeXT's version of the tools appear next to corresponding screen snapshots—not in the main body. However, on other platforms, the steps are nearly identical although the tools may look different (refer to your manual for more details).

The developer tools used in this chapter are:

❑   *Project Builder*, a tool for managing all project related files and compiling and debugging source code.

❑   *Interface Builder*, a tool for building Graphical User Interfaces (GUIs), and creating subclasses and source code "stubs."

The OpenStep frameworks used in this chapter are:

❑   *Foundation Kit*, a framework containing all the basic classes, most importantly the NSObject root class. Other classes are used to create strings, numbers, dates, arrays, and dictionaries. It also contains classes in support of Distributed Objects, the release mechanism, archiving and encoding, exception handling, and the notification center.

❑   *Application Kit*, a framework for building GUIs. It contains classes used to create user interface components such as windows, panels, buttons, text fields, menus, and text documents. You primarily manipulate instances of Application Kit classes when using Interface Builder.

This chapter also contains Booch Lite diagrams and Objective-C code. If you are unfamiliar with these, refer to Appendix C—*Booch Lite* and Appendix B—*Objective-C*, respectively.

This chapter focuses on the Cards basic responsibilities, outlined during analysis (see Chapter 4—*Analysis*), which is suitable for the first iteration. This functionality includes providing an index, creating agents, changing the name of agents, adding and removing collaborators, deleting agents, and saving and loading agents. Implementing these basic functions poses some interesting problems, such as synchronizing the views using the notification center. Group collaboration, outlined in the second iteration of analysis, will be covered in Chapter 7—*Distributed Objects*.

Note, this chapter purposely does not cover every detail of the implementation—refer to Appendix D—*Class Specifications* and the source code on the enclosed disk for the complete implementation of Cards.

Reviewing Output of Design

Use the output of OO design as a guide during implementation. The output of design consists mostly of diagrams:

❑   *Class diagrams* document class hierarchies.

❑   *Object diagrams* document part-whole relationships and message flow.

❑   *Interaction diagrams* also capture message flow.

❑   *Class category diagrams* document groupings of classes into modules.

❑   *Process diagrams* document the architecture of applications and processes.

The output may also include class specifications, some code (that is, Objective-C class interface files), and user interface snapshots (that is, Interface Builder nib files).

Most of the Cards application classes were discovered during the design stage. Refer to Chapter 5—*Design* for these figures:

❑   Figure 5–2—*Index-Agent class diagram with control objects* identifies the entity objects Agent and Index and control objects ControlIndex and ControlAgent.

❑   The interfaces to these objects are revealed in Figure 5–4—*Interactive diagram for changing the name of an agent*, 5–5—*Object diagram for adding a collaborator*, and Figure 5–6—*Interaction diagram for deleting an agent*.

Even the initial Objective-C interface file for the Agent class was created during design. However, few of the interface objects (windows and views in OpenStep) were documented, so there's plenty of room for creativity when designing the user interface.

Creating the Cards Project

Before you write a single line of code, you need to create the Cards project using Project Builder. Project Builder helps you organize and access all your files. It is the central application used for editing files, compiling, and debugging. You can launch the other developer tools by clicking on files and buttons in Project Builder, so keep your project file open at all times.

Figure 6–1   Creating the Cards project.

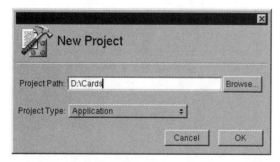

1. Launch Project Builder.

2. Choose New from the Project menu. The New Project panel will appear.

3. Browse to the directory where you want the Cards project to reside.

4. On Windows, type the path, ending with Cards, in the Project Path field. On Mach, type the name of the application, Cards, in the Name field.

5. Choose Application from the Project Type pop-up list.

6. Click the OK button.

Create the Cards project now as shown in Figure 6–1. The Cards project window will appear as shown in Figure 6–2. Project Builder creates the initial files and directories needed to compile, link, and run your application. Project Builder organizes these files and directories into groups called *suitcases*. The project window contains a browser to navigate through these suitcases. (Note that the suitcases do not correspond to subdirectories in the Cards directory.) On NeXT's version, there's also a Frameworks suitcase for easily browsing OpenStep header files and documentation.

You'll find the **main()** function in a file called **Cards_main.m** in the Other Sources suitcase. This file and **Makefile**, located in the Supporting File suitcase, are automatically generated by Project Builder and should not be modified directly. You customize your build by modifying **Makefile.preamble** and **Makefile.postamble**, but you rarely need to do so.

The main nib file, **Cards.nib**, is located in the Interfaces suitcase. This is an Interface Builder document that contains the application's *main menu* (the window menu bar on Microsoft Windows platforms or the menu that appears in the upper left hand corner of the screen on other platforms), and any other windows and objects that are created when you launch the application.

Figure 6–2   Cards project window.

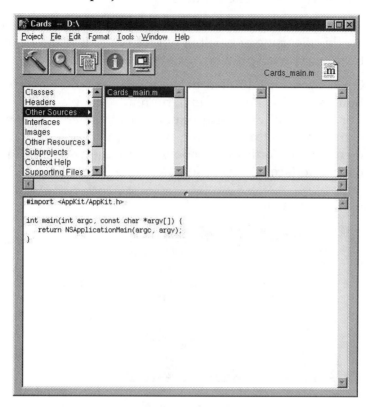

Creating the Index

You need to think about how you want the user interface to look and behave. If you are programming while reading this chapter, you can be as creative as you like designing the interface objects. As long as you keep the same control and entity object interfaces, the rest of the implementation presented in this book will still apply.

In this example, a view of the index will be displayed at all times, so that the user can easily select and open cards. First, you'll create the entity object for the index called Index. Next, you'll create a control object for the entire application that will create the index. Finally, you'll create the corresponding index control and interface objects.

Creating the Index Class

You need to create the source file for the Index entity object. You can create this file using any editor, but it's easier if Interface Builder creates it for you, especially if you are unfamiliar with Objective-C.

Open **Cards.nib**, located in the Interfaces suitcase, to launch Interface Builder if its not already running (double-click **Cards.nib**). The **Cards.nib** window will appear. If you already have interface files for the entity objects created during the design stage, you can drag and drop them on the **Cards.nib** window now. Otherwise, you can create classes using Interface Builder following the steps in Figure 6–3.

Figure 6–3   Creating Index.

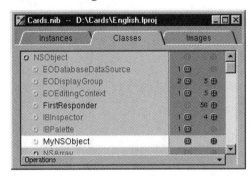

1. Click the Classes tab and select NSObject from the list of classes.

2. Choose Subclass from the Operations pull-down list.

3. A new class will appear in the list called MyNSObject. Change the name of the object to Index.

To the right of the class name you should see two small buttons: ▣ is the symbol for outlets and ▦ is the symbol for actions. Each is annotated with the number of outlets and actions respectively (including inherited outlets and actions).

Outlets and actions have specific meanings to Interface Builder. An *outlet* is any instance variable, typed **id** (that is, a reference to some application object). An *action* is any method with the following signature (for example, a callback method for NSButton):

```
- (void)anyMethod:(id)sender;
```

Interface Builder finds the outlets and actions for a particular class by reading its interface file. You will learn more about outlets and actions when making connections in *Creating ControlIndex*.

Although outlets and actions have specific meanings to Interface Builder, they are implemented as just instance variables and methods. Taking advantage of this fact, you can create an outlet for each Index instance variable and an action for each method. Refer to the initial interface file created during design, and create the following outlets as described in Figure 6–4:

```
agents
```

Create the following actions as described in Figure 6–4:

```
addAgent:
agents
removeAgent:
willDelete:
```

Notice that outlets are of type **id** and actions take a single argument *sender*. Therefore, a ":" for the argument is appended to each action, regardless of what you attempt to type. Some of Index's instance variables are not intended to be **id** and some methods are not intended to be real actions—they have no arguments—so you'll need to edit the source files later.

Figure 6–4   Adding outlets.

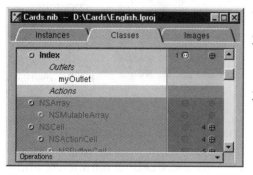

1. Click the 🔘 button.

2. Choose Add Outlet from the Operations pull-down list (or press Return twice).

3. Change the name of the outlet to **agents**.

Figure 6–5   Adding actions.

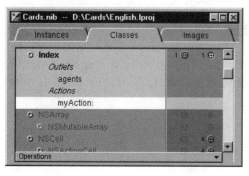

1. Click the 🔘 button.

2. Choose Add Action from the Operations pull-down list (or press Return twice).

3. Change the name of the action to **addAgent:**.

4. Repeat these steps to add remaining actions.

When you are done creating all the outlets and actions, you can close the outlets and actions by clicking their buttons. Save **Cards.nib** (choose Save from the File or Document menu).

Now you are ready to create the source files for Index and add them to the project as described in Figure 6–6. After doing this you can see that **Index.m** and **Index.h** were added to the Cards project Classes and Headers suitcases respectively (you should still have Project Builder running). By clicking on these files you will see the source code, displayed below, ready for editing or double-click to open them in an editor. Go to the Cards project directory and you will see that the source files were placed there.

Figure 6–6   Creating Index source files.

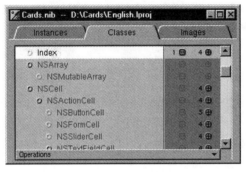

1. Select Index.

2. Choose Create Files from the Operations pull-down list.

3. A panel will appear confirming this action. Click YES.

4. Another panel will appear asking if you want these files to be inserted in the Cards project. Click YES.

Now you need to customize the Index source files—fix instance variable types, fix method arguments, and add method implementations. You also need to override **init** and **dealloc** to initialize and release an index's instance variables respectively. (See Chapter 5—*Design* for a description of the release mechanism).

Go to Project Builder and select **Index.h** from the Headers suitcase and edit the file identical to the listing below. Add declarations for **init** and **dealloc**. Remove the arguments from the **agents** method and change the return value to **id.Index.h** should look like the following:

```
#import <AppKit/AppKit.h>

@interface Index : NSObject
{
    id agents;
}
- (id)init;
- (void)dealloc;
- (void)addAgent:(Agent *)anAgent;
- (id)agents;
- (void)removeAgent:(Agent *)anAgent;
- (void)willDelete:(NSNotification *)notification;
@end
```

init is used to initialize the receiver's instance variables, and **dealloc** is used to release them. Index's **willDelete:** method is the callback for notification if an agent is deleted. **willDelete:** removes the agent from its **agents** array. How this works is explained later in *Deleting Agents*.

Next, you need to update the corresponding method implementations in **Index.m**. It's easy to do this if you double-click on **Index.h** to open it in a separate window. Then, display **Index.m** in the project window. Now you can select the method signatures from the interface file and paste them into the implementation file. This is a bit laborious, but better than typing in the file from scratch. Save **Index.m**.

NSObject is the root class of most objects with very few exceptions (for example, NSProxy). The advantage of having a root class is that all objects inherit basic functionality and they can participate in larger reusable designs called mechanisms. Remember, a *mechanism* is a design that specifies how a collection of objects cooperate to provide some service. The most commonly used mechanism in OpenStep is the initialization and deallocation mechanisms.

The *initialization mechanism* ensures that all instance variables are initialized in the proper order. Subclasses of NSObject inherit the **alloc**... class methods and **init** instance method which together allocate memory for a new instance and initialize its instance variables (for example, initializes the **isa** pointer). It's important that superclass initialization takes place before subclass initialization. In this way, the initialization mechanism works as a waterfall, initializing the instance variables defined by the root class first, followed by instance variables defined by its subclass, and so on, until all the receiver's instance variables are initialized.

However, the **init** method has no arguments and therefore may not be suitable for all types of initialization. If you need to create another initialization method, the convention in OpenStep is to begin the method with **init**, followed by keywords for its arguments (for example, NSView's **initWithFrame:** method). Typically, the **init...** method with the most arguments is the designated initializer. The *designated initializer* is the method that all other **init...** methods should invoke as part of their implementation to properly initialize the instance. For example, **init** is the designated initializer for NSObject, and **initWithFrame:** is the designated initializer for NSView.

It is important to know which methods are the designated initializers if you subclass OpenStep classes. If you define a new designated initializer (one that takes more arguments), you need to override all inherited designated initializers to invoke this new **init...** method as part of its implementation. If you do not cover all the inherited designated initializers, then invoking inherited methods (like NSArray's **array** class method) may not return valid objects. If you simply subclass NSObject, then you only have to worry about overriding the **init** method.

Therefore, when you create subclasses of NSObject, you should override the **init** method to invoke super's **init** first and then initialize the receiver's instance variables, as in this implementation of Index's **init** method:

```
- (id)init
{
    [super init];
    agents = [[NSMutableArray array] retain];
    return self;
}
```

Add this method implementation to **Index.m**.

The *deallocation mechanism* is the inverse of the initialization mechanism—it deallocates instances in reverse order by deallocating instance variables defined by the receiver's class first, then the inherited class and up the class hierarchy until it reaches the root class. Classes derived from NSObject inherit the **dealloc** method that performs the final deallocation by freeing the instance's object structure.

If you create a subclass of NSObject and override the designated initializer or create a new one that creates new objects or C structures, you also need to override **dealloc**. You implement dealloc to release all instance variables and structures defined by the receiver's class, and then invoke **super**'s dealloc.

Note, in all other cases, you never invoke **dealloc** directly. The **release** method (also inherited from NSObject) will eventually invoke **dealloc** when the receiver's reference count reaches zero. See Chapter 5—*Design* for details on how the release mechanism works.

Therefore, each designated initializer needs an inverse method that releases all dynamically created instance variables and structures as in Index's **dealloc** method. Add this implementation to **Index.m**:

```
- (void)dealloc
{
    [agents release];
    [super dealloc];
    return;
}
```

Always remember to keep the **init** and **dealloc** methods up-to-date when you add instance variables.

Implement the **agents** method to return the **agents** instance variable. The implementation of **willDelete:** is covered in *Deleting Agents*, and **addAgent:** and **removeAgent:** is covered in *Adding and Removing Agents from the Index*.

Creating ControlApp

The index needs to be created when the application is first launched. An NSApplication's delegate is designed to handle this type of setup when the application is launched and cleanup when the application is terminated (if necessary). You'll also need an object that is the target of action messages sent by the main menu (a *target* is the recipient of a UI object's action message). This object can also act as the NSApplication's delegate and is called ControlApp because it's a control object for the entire application.

Open the main nib file **Cards.nib** from the Interfaces suitcase in Project Builder—this will launch Interface Builder if it's not already running. Using Interface Builder, create a new class called ControlApp as a subclass of NSObject (follow same steps in Figure 6–3—*Creating Index*). Then add an **index** outlet and **newAgent:** action method (to be used later). Create the ControlApp source files and add them to the project.

Using Interface Builder, create an instance of ControlApp as shown in Figure 6–7. The Instances folder will automatically be displayed and contain a new object labeled ControlApp. (You've just added an instance of ControlApp to the main nib file, so when the application launches and loads the main nib, an instance of ControlApp is created.)

Figure 6–7   Creating a ControlApp instance.

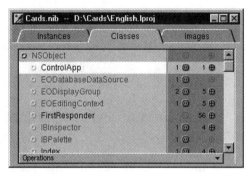

1. Click on the Classes tab.

2. Select ControlApp.

3. Choose Instantiate from the Operations pull-down list.

Next, inspect the File's Owner as described in Figure 6–8. You will see that the File's Owner is specified as an instance of NSApplication. All nib files are read and owned by an object called *File's Owner*. All interface objects are stored in nib files, so the File's Owner acts as the intermediary between these objects and entity objects. The File's Owner is a classic control object. When the main nib file is loaded, the File's Owner is set to a global instance of NSApplication called **NSApp**.

Figure 6–8   Inspecting the File's Owner.

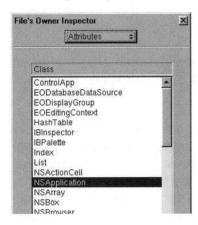

1. Select the File's Owner object in the Instances folder.

2. Choose Inspector from the Tools menu.

3. Choose Attributes from the pop-up list in the File's Owner Inspector window.

Now go back to Interface Builder and set **NSApp**'s delegate to the instance of ControlApp as shown in Figure 6–9. Save **Cards.nib**.

Figure 6–9   Connecting **NSApp**'s delegate.

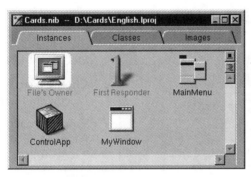

1. Click the Instances tab.

2. Control-drag from the File's Owner icon to the ControlApp icon.

3. The File's Owner Inspector window will appear with the delegate outlet selected. Click Connect.

This enables you to override NSApplication's delegate method **applicationDidFinishLaunching:** to initialize ControlApp's **index** instance variable. This task isn't so easy, because there are several components to the index, as you will discover below.

Creating ControlIndex

You could place the interface objects for the index in MyWindow, the application's main window displayed in the Instances folder (automatically created by Interface Builder), but there's a more elegant *modular* way to implement the index. Even though there is only one index per

Cards application, it's a good idea to build it as a reusable component that could be used in other applications—you never know what future requirements will be.

While you have **Cards.nib** open and the Instances folder displayed, remove MyWindow (select MyWindow and choose Delete from the Edit menu). Save **Cards.nib**.

Interface Builder supports reusable components called *modules*. When you create a module, you can specify the File's Owner to be an instance of your class. The File's Owner will be a control object that acts as the intermediary between the interface objects and entity object. The design stage also revealed the need for an index control object, called ControlIndex. Therefore, create a module for an index's interface objects as shown in Figure 6–10. You save the file as **ControlIndex.nib** since it will be owned by ControlIndex.

Figure 6–10 Creating ControlIndex.nib.

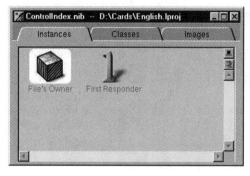

1. Choose File→New Module→New Empty from the main menu (on Mach, its Document→New).

2. Choose Save As from the File or Document menu.

3. Type ControlIndex in the Filename or Name field and click Save or OK.

4. When asked if the file should be added to the project, click YES.

Now, create the index interface objects needed to display the list of agents as shown in Figure 6–11. In this example, the index only displays the title attribute using an NSTableView. More columns can be added later to the table to display other information such as the author's name and date last modified. (NSTableView and NSColumnView are additions to OpenStep. If these classes are not available on your platform, use a similar object such as NSMatrix.)

Figure 6–11 Creating index interface objects.

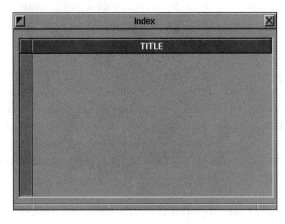

1. Drag off an NSWindow from of the Windows palette.

2. Change the window's title to Index using the Window Inspector.

3. Drag an NSScrollView containing an NSTableView from the TabulationViews palette and drop it in the window.

4. Resize the scrollview and window.

5. Remove unwanted columns and add titles to and resize remaining columns.

Next, you need to create the ControlIndex class as a subclass of NSObject, specifying its outlets and actions using Interface Builder. ControlIndex will need access to each user interface object, so add outlets:

```
table
titleColumn
window
```

All control objects need access to their models, so add another outlet called **model**.

Now add action methods:

```
ok:
revert:
open:
```

These methods will be invoked by interface and entity objects. The **ok:** action method confirms user changes to **model**, and **revert:** changes the user interface to reflect **model**. The **open:** action method opens a card (when the user double-clicks its entry in the table). When done, create the source files for ControlIndex and add them to the project. Save **ControlIndex.nib**.

Change the File's Owner to an instance of ControlIndex (follow same steps as shown in Figure 6–8, then select ControlIndex from the list of classes).

Make connections between the File's Owner and the interface objects as shown in Figure 6–12. Remember, you always control-drag from the source to the destination object. Connect the File's Owner **table** outlet to the NSTableView (the object inside the NSScrollView). Similarly, connect the **titleColumn** outlet to the NSTableColumn by control-dragging to the column's header. Connect the **window** outlet to the NSWindow by control-dragging to the Window icon in the Instances folder. Don't connect **model**—it will be set later.

Note, when you make a connection using Interface Builder, that connection is stored in the nib file. The assignment is actually made later at runtime when the nib file is loaded.

Similarly, you need to make connections from the interface objects to the File's Owner. This time you control-drag from the interface object to the File's Owner.

NSTableView has a **dataSource** outlet used to fill the table with data. Connect the table's **dataSource** outlet to the File's Owner (you need to double-click the table to select it before control-dragging). Later, you'll see how **dataSource** works. Save **ControlIndex.nib**.

Figure 6–12 Making connections.

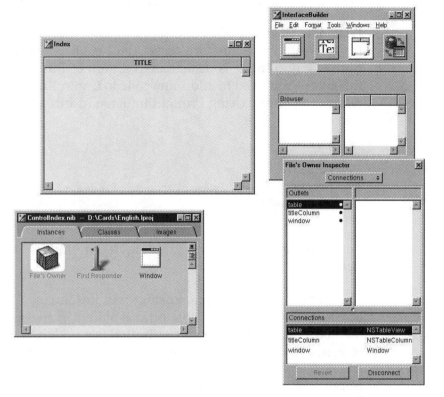

1. Click the Instances tab and control-drag from the File's Owner object to an interface object.

2. Select Connections from the pop-up list in the Inspector. The inspector will contain a list of all the outlets for the source object in the left-hand column, and all the actions for the destination object in the right-hand column.

3. Select the outlet that corresponds to the interface object and click Connect.

Before leaving Interface Builder, set **table**'s attributes using the NSTable-View Inspector (double-click the table, open the Inspector, and choose Attributes from the pop-up list). Allow empty and multiple selections, and don't allow reordering (the index will sort the agents alphabetically). You can also turn off the horizontal scroller. Now, select the column (click the table header) and turn off the Editable option. Save **ControlIndex.nib**.

Normally, you use Interface Builder to set the targets and actions for each interface object. Unfortunately, not all target/actions can be set using Interface Builder, in which case, you need to add some code to the File's Owner designated initializer as shown below.

First, new instances of ControlIndex need to load the **ControlIndex.nib** file to create these interface objects and connections at runtime (every time a ControlIndex is instantiated). Interface Builder doesn't generate this code—you need to add some code to ControlIndex's designated initializer to do this. Using Project Builder, add **init** to **ControlIndex.m** as in:

```
- (id)init
{
    [super init];
    [NSBundle loadNibNamed:@"ControlIndex.nib" owner:self];
    return self;
}
```

Remember to add the corresponding declaration for **init** to **ControlIndex.h**.

NSBundle's **loadNibNamed:owner:** will instantiate all of the interface objects and make all the connections stored in the nib file. After this method is invoked, most of ControlIndex's outlets will be set to valid objects, and **awakeFromNib:** is sent to the File's Owner.

Implement **awakeFromNib:** to set more interface object attributes. Code is added to allow selection of agents, and to set the target/action for **table** when an agent is double-clicked (this action will open an agent's card) as in:

```
- (void)awakeFromNib
{
    [table setAutoresizesAllColumnsToFit:YES];
    [table setTarget:self];
    [table setDoubleAction:@selector(open:)];
    return;
}
```

Don't forget to implement **dealloc** as well. In this implementation, ControlIndex's **window** is closed (and released by default), removing it from the screen and releasing its views:

```
- (void)dealloc
{
    [window performClose:self]; /* Notifies delegate. */
    [super dealloc];
    return;
}
```

Note, you do not have to release ControlIndex's outlets, because they were not retained when the nib file was loaded (remember these connections were made using Interface Builder). In general, only the owner of an object should retain it. Views are owned by their superviews and the root view is owned by its window, so these objects are all released when the window is released. The Application Kit is consistent with this ownership policy. For example, targets and delegates (your application objects) are not owned by Application Kit objects and therefore are not retained. Also, **model** was not released because it was not retained, see **setModel:** below.

Finally, you're ready to override NSApplication's delegate method, **applicationDidFinishLaunching:**, to display the index when the application is first launched. Add the following implementation to **ControlApp.m** and corresponding declaration to **ControlApp.h**:

```
- (void)applicationDidFinishLaunching:
        (NSNotification *)notification
{
    id controller;

    index = [Index new];
    controller = [[ControlIndex new] setModel:index];
    [[controller window] makeKeyAndOrderFront:self];
    return;
}
```

To complete the ControlIndex implementation, you need to implement the following methods: **model**, **setModel:**, **window,** and **revert:**. The **model** and **window** methods are simply get methods that return their respective instance variables.

Note, **setModel:** purposely doesn't retain its **model**, because the ControlIndex object doesn't own it (the ControlIndex will be notified when its **model** is deallocated similar to *Deleting Agents*—see source code for details). The **setModel:** method simply maintains a reference to the new model and reverts its interface objects to the state of the new model as in:

```
- (id)setModel:(id)anObject
{
    model = anObject;
    [self revert:self];
    return self;
}
```

revert: should load the table with **model**'s list of agents. This is done by sending **reloadData** to **table**:

```
- (void)revert:(id)sender
{
    [table reloadData];
    return;
}
```

Note, an NSTableView gets the data it displays from its **dataSource** where **dataSource** is expected to conform to the NSTableDataSource informal protocol. It's not necessary to implement all methods in this protocol, just **numberOfRowsInTableView:** to return the number of rows and **tableView:objectValueForTableColumn:row:** to return the value at a particular column and row. By implementing this protocol, the table is automatically propagated with data, and you do not have to worry about how the data is displayed.

Earlier, using Interface Builder, **table**'s **dataSource** was set to the File's Owner, an instance of ControlIndex. Therefore, all you need to do for this mechanism to work is implement ControlIndex's **numberOfRows-InTableView:** and **tableView:objectValueForTableColumn:row:** methods as in:

```
- (int)numberOfRowsInTableView:(NSTableView *)tableView
{
    return (model ? [[model agents] count] : 0);
}
```

```
- (id)tableView:(NSTableView *)tableView
    objectValueForTableColumn:(NSTableColumn *)tableColumn
    row:(int)row
{
    if (tableColumn == titleColumn)
        return [[[model agents] objectAtIndex:row] title];
    return nil;
}
```

Add the above methods to **ControlIndex.m** and corresponding declarations to **ControlIndex.h**. The **ok:** and **open:** methods will be implemented later.

Creating Agents

The index will first appear empty, so the user needs some way to create agents and add them to the index. You'll do this by adding a menu item to the main menu. When an agent is first created, its card is displayed so the user can change agent attributes. Since you want to mimic paper index cards as much as possible, there will be one card per agent where cards can be displayed independently and freely arranged on the workspace. If the user closes a card, it can be reopened by double-clicking on its name in the index.

Creating the Agent Class

To create the source files for the Agent entity object, follow the same steps for creating Index in *Creating the Index Class* above. The instance variables and methods for the Agent class were derived during design in Chapter 5 and documented in this interface file:

```
#import <AppKit/AppKit.h>

@interface Agent : NSObject
{
    id collaborators;
    NSMutableString *responsibilities;
    NSMutableString *title;
}
- (id)init;
- (void)dealloc;
- (void)addCollaborators:(NSArray *)anArray;
- (id)collaborators;
- (void)delete;
- (void)removeCollaborators:(NSArray *)anArray;
- (NSString *)responsibilities;
- (void)setResponsibilities:(NSString *)aString;
- (void)setTitle:(NSString *)aString;
- (NSString *)title;
- (void)willDelete:(NSNotification *)notification;
@end
```

Use Interface Builder to open **Cards.nib** and create the Agent class. Add the **collaborators**, **responsibilities** and **title** outlets and methods listed above to the Agent class. Create the Agent source files and edit **Agent.h** identical to the listing above. Update the method signatures in **Agent.m** accordingly.

Implement the **init** method to initialize the instance variables and the **dealloc** method to release them.

Note that the method names **title** and **setTitle:** are already used by the Application Kit. In Objective-C, all methods with the same name must have the same method signature or else the correct method implementation may not be found at runtime. The Application Kit method signatures suit our purposes as well, since **title** and **responsibilities** will be instances of NSString (NSMutableString to be exact).

Implement the get methods (**collaborators, responsibilities,** and **title**) to return their respective instance variables, and set methods (**setTitle:** and **setResponsibilities:**) to set their respective instance variables as in:

```
- (void)setTitle:(NSString *)aString
{
    [title setString:aString];
    return;
}

- (NSString *)title
{
    return title;
}
```

delete is invoked by a control object to "delete" the receiver. Agent's **willDelete:** method is the callback for notification if a collaborator is deleted. **willDelete:** removes the collaborator from its list which will send **release** to the collaborator. You don't need to implement these methods yet, they are explained, along with the release mechanism, in *Deleting Agents*.

The methods **addCollaborators:** and **removeCollaborators:** will also be implemented later in *Adding and Removing Collaborators*.

Modifying the Main Menu

You need to add a menu item to the main menu for creating new agents. This is done by creating a Cards submenu with a New menu item as shown in Figure 6–13.

Figure 6–13 Modifying the main menu.

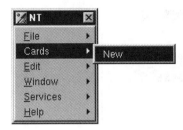

1. Open Cards.nib.

2. Click on the Instances tab and double-click on the MainMenu icon to display the menu.

3. Drag Submenu from the Menus palette and drop it on the main menu. This will add a new submenu containing one item.

4. Change the name of the submenu to Cards, and change the name of its menu item to New (click the Cards submenu to open it).

The ControlApp instance (created earlier) will be the target for this menu item. The main menu sends the action message to the target when that menu item is selected. So, connect the New menu item to the ControlApp instance, and select the **newAgent:** action, as you did earlier when making connections (control-drag from the New menu item to the ControlApp instance). ControlApp's **newAgent:** method (implemented later) will create and display a new card, and add it to the index. Save **Cards.nib**.

Creating ControlAgent

Cards will be created on-the-fly and therefore can't simply be added to the main nib file as was done with the ControlApp instance above. The best way to implement a card is to create a module type nib file using Interface Builder. You need to create a module for an agent's user interface and specify the File's Owner as an instance of ControlAgent. Follow the same steps for creating **ControlIndex.nib** above (see Figure 6–10): launch Interface Builder, create a new module, save the file as **ControlAgent.nib**, and add it to the project.

Now, create the interface objects to display and allow editing of an agent's attributes as shown in Figure 6–14. Note, the layout of this computerized CRC card is different from Cunningham and Beck to better suit the OpenStep user interface. Also, NSTableView is an addition to OpenStep. If it is not available on your platform, use a similar object such as NSMatrix.

Figure 6–14 Creating agent interface objects.

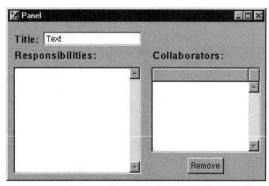

1. Drag a NSWindow or NSPanel from of the Windows palette and drop it on the desktop (on Microsoft Windows all NSWindows contain the main menu, so use NSPanel instead).

2. Drag a NSTextField from the Views palette to contain the agent's title and drop it on the window. Increase the text field size to accommodate long names.

3. Drag a Title from the Views palette for a Title label and change the font size.

4. Duplicate the later NSTextField and change its text to Responsibilities. Duplicate it again and change its text to Collaborators.

5. Drag a NSScrollView from the DataViews palette for the responsibilities text.

6. Drag a NSScrollView containing an NSTableView from the TabulationViews palette for the collaborators list.

7. Only one column is needed for listing collaborators, so double-click the second column and delete it. Resize remaining column to fit.

8. Choose Inspector from the Tools menu, select the collaborators tableview, and change its attributes to allow empty and multiple selections. Also disallow reordering and remove the horizontal scrollbar.

9. Resize window and scrollviews and position titles above scrollviews.

10. Drag a Button from the Views palette. Change the text to Remove and place it below the collaborators list.

Next you need to create the ControlAgent class, specifying its outlets and actions using Interface Builder. Again, follow the same steps for creating ControlIndex above: subclass NSObject, change the name of the subclass to ControlAgent, create an outlet for each interface object (**collaboratorTable**, **collaboratorColumn**, **removeButton**, **responsibilities**, **title**, and **window**), add another outlet called **model**, and add action methods to be invoked by user interface objects (**ok:**, **open:**, **removeCollaborators:** and **revert:**).

Similar to ControlIndex, the **ok:** action method confirms user changes to **model**, and **revert:** changes the user interface to reflect **model**. The **open:** action method opens collaborator cards, and **removeCollaborators:** will remove the selected collaborators. Create the corresponding source files and add them to the project. Save **ControlAgent.nib**.

Change the File's Owner to an instance of ControlAgent, and make connections between the File's Owner and interface objects:

❏ Connect **title** to the NSTextField that displays the agent's title.

❏ Connect **responsibilities** to the NSTextView inside the NSScroll-View.

❏ Connect **collaboratorTable** to the NSTableView inside the collaborators scrollview.

❏ Connect **collaboratorColumn** to the single NSTableColumn in the scrollview (control-drag to the column's header).

❏ Connect **removeButton** to the Remove button.

❏ Connect the Window object to the **window** outlet.

The **model** outlet will be set at runtime.

Now set the targets and actions for each user interface object. In this example, ControlAgent is the target for the user interface objects. For example, when the **title** text changes, the **ok:** action should be invoked. Also, when the Remove button is clicked, the **removeCollaborators:** action should be invoked. After making these connections, save **ControlAgent.nib**.

Similar to creating **ControlIndex.nib**, you also need to connect **collaboratorTable**'s **dataSource** outlet to the File's Owner (again, double-click the NSScrollView containing the NSTableView to select it before control-dragging). Later you'll add the NSDataSourceTable informal protocol methods to ControlAgent so that **collaboratorTable** displays the list of collaborators.

Again, some targets, actions, and attributes can't be set using Interface Builder, so you'll need to add some code to the designated initializer and override **awakeFromNib:** as shown below. New instances of ControlAgent need to load the **ControlAgent.nib** file to create these interface objects and connections. Remember Interface Builder doesn't generate this code—you need to add some code to ControlAgent's designated initializer as in:

```
- (id)init
{
    [super init];
    [NSBundle loadNibNamed:@"ControlAgent.nib" owner:self];
    return self;
}
```

After **loadNibNamed:owner:** is invoked, ControlAgent's outlets will be set to valid objects, and **awakeFromNib:** is invoked. Override **awake-FromNib:** to set more interface object attributes. For example, code is added to set the target and action of **collaboratorTable** when an item is double-clicked as in:

```
- (void)awakeFromNib
{
    [responsibilities setDelegate:self];
    [collaboratorTable setTarget:self];
    [collaboratorTable setDoubleAction:@selector(open:)];
    return;
}
```

Again, don't forget to implement the **dealloc** method. ControlAgent's **dealloc** implementation should release its **window** and **model** as in:

```
- (void)dealloc
{
    [window performClose:self]; /* Notifies delegate. */
    [super dealloc];
    return;
}
```

Remember, you don't have to release ControlIndex's outlets, because they were not retained when the nib file was loaded. The **window** outlet owns all its views, and they will be released when the window is released. Similarly, **model** is not released because it was not retained (see **setModel:** below).

Finally, you can implement ControlApp's **newAgent:** method to create a new agent, add it to the index, create its controller, and display its window. Add the following implementation to **ControlApp.m**:

```
- (void)newAgent:(id)sender
{
    id agent, controller;
```

```
/* Create a new agent and add it to the index. */
agent = [Agent new];
[index addAgent:agent];

/* Create a controller and display its window. */
controller = [[ControlAgent new] setModel:agent];
[[controller window] makeKeyAndOrderFront:self];

return;
}
```

Remember, ControlApp has an instance variable **index** that was set to an instance of Index in **applicationDidFinishLaunching:**.

To finish up this step, you need to add the methods **model** and **setModel:** to ControlAgent to return and set the model. Also, add a method **window** to simply return ControlAgent's **window** instance variable. The **setModel:** method should change the model and revert the user interface objects to the state of **model** as in:

```
- (id)setModel:(id)anObject
{
    model = anObject;
    [self revert:self];
    return self;
}
```

Note, that model is not retained because it is not owned by this instance. This instance will be notified when the model is deallocated similar to *Deleting Agents* (see source code for details).

Also, implement **revert:** to change **title**'s text, **responsibilities**'s text, and **window**'s title as in:

```
- (void)revert:(id)sender
{
    [title setStringValue:[model title]];
    [responsibilities setString:[model responsibilities]];
    [window setTitle:[model title]];
    [collaboratorTable reloadData];
    return;
}
```

revert: also reloads the data in **collaboratorTable**. **collaboratorTable**'s **dataSource** outlet was connected to this instance of ControlAgent; therefore, all you need to do for this mechanism to work is implement the following NSDataSourceTable methods:

```
- (int)numberOfRowsInTableView:(NSTableView *)tableView
{
    return (model ? [[model collaborators] count] : 0);
}

- (id)tableView:(NSTableView *)tableView
    objectValueForTableColumn:(NSTableColumn *)tableColumn
    row:(int)row
{
    if (tableColumn == collaboratorColumn)
        return [[[model collaborators] objectAtIndex:row] title];
    return nil;
}
```

Add the above methods to **ControlAgent.m** and corresponding declarations to **ControlAgent.h**.

Compiling and Running the Application

Although you are not done, its a good time to take a break from writing code to compile and run the program. This way you can catch syntax errors early and incrementally test your implementation.

Before compiling the program, you should tie up loose ends. For example, make sure **Index.h** imports **Agent.h**, and **ControlApp.m** imports **Index.h**, **ControlIndex.h**, and **ControlAgent.h**. Also, **ControlIndex.m** needs to import **Index.h**, and **ControlAgent.m** needs to import **Agent.h**.

Compile a version of Cards following these steps:

❑ Launch Project Builder, and open the Project Build panel by clicking the hammer button.

❑ Open the Build Options panel by clicking the check mark button (Options button on some platforms).

❑ Choose debug from the Target pop-up list.

❑ Close the Build Options panel.

❑ Click the hammer button on the Project Build panel (BUILD button on some platforms).

If done correctly, the status display reads "Building Cards.debug."

After you have successfully compiled Cards, run the debugger by clicking the launch button (the computer monitor icon) in the project window and then clicking the spray can in the Launch panel (on some platforms, just click the spray can). Click the play button to run the application.

The index should appear when the application is first launched. Choose New from the Cards window to create an agent. Notice that the new card doesn't appear in the index, and if you change the name of the agent, the window's title doesn't change. This is because entity objects, instances of Index and Agent, are not notifying their control objects of changes to their state. Instances of ControlIndex and ControlAgent need to update interface objects when entity objects change. Also, you haven't fully implemented adding and removing collaborators or deleting agents. These features will be addressed next.

Adding and Removing Agents from the Index

At this point you implemented some basic functionality and learned how to use the programming tools along the way. Now you are ready to implement more interesting aspects of Cards, synchronizing entity and interface objects, and updating other links between objects. For example, when you create a new agent, it should automatically appear in the index.

As discovered during design, OpenStep's notification center is ideal for updating these types of object links. The *notification center* is a mechanism for broadcasting notifications from one object to many objects. In the Cards design, any interested object will add itself as an observer of change notifications sent by entity objects. Specifically, in this section, the ControlIndex instance adds itself as an observer of notifications sent by its model, an instance of Index.

Adding and removing agents from the index was not addressed during design, so you need to model this behavior first before writing any code. The implementation of ControlApp's **newAgent:** method (presented above) sends **addAgent:** to its **index**, passing the new instance of Agent. Assume **addAgent:** posts a notification, and ControlIndex previously added itself as an observer of this notification specifying **indexDidAddAgent:** as the callback. The interaction diagram shown in Figure 6–15 documents the rest of the message flow. This design is similar to that of changing the name of an agent which was covered during design (see Figure 5–4—*Interaction digram for changing the name of an agent*).

Figure 6–15 First interaction diagram for adding new agents.

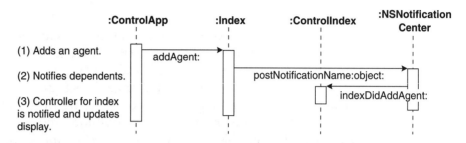

However, upon closer inspection you will find that the actions of adding an agent, adding a collaborator, and changing the name of an agent have something else in common. In all these cases, either the index's **agents** or the agent's **collaborators** needs to be re-ordered alphabetically. Therefore, not only is one entry in the array changed but possibly the whole array is affected. Using this fact, you can considerably simplify the design by reducing the number of notifications posed by the index and the number of callback methods.

Note, don't be afraid to change the design when you find flaws, especially if you can simplify it. The output of the design stage is intended as a guide, not a bible, for the implementation stage!

Since the entire **agents** array may be affected by adding a new agent to the index, its control object will need to update the whole table, not just one entry. The updated interaction diagram is shown in Figure 6–16, where ControlIndex's **indexDidChangeAgents:** method handles all types of changes to **agents**. The index will post an IndexDidChangeAgents-Notification when ever **agents** changes (that is, when an agent is added or removed, or when an agent's name changed causing the array to be reordered).

Figure 6–16 Second interaction diagram for adding new agents.

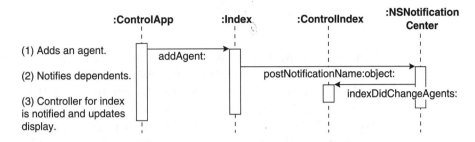

Now step through this diagram to implement the behavior of adding a new card to the index. Removing a card from the index is similar, so you'll implement these behaviors together.

First, you create a notification name for each type of notification. Notification names are just NSString objects, so add this code to **Index.m**:

```
NSString *IndexDidChangeAgentsNotification =
    @"IndexDidChangeAgentsNotification";
```

Then, add an external declaration for this notification name to **Index.h**, as in:

```
extern NSString *IndexDidChangeAgentsNotification;
```

For this mechanism to work, first the ControlIndex instance needs to add itself as observers of this notification. The best place to do this is when its model is set, so modify ControlIndex's **setModel:** as follows:

```
- setModel:anObject
{
    /* Unregister for notifications from the old model. */
    if (model){
        [[NSNotificationCenter defaultCenter]
            removeObserver:self
            name:IndexDidChangeAgentsNotification
            object:model];
    }

    model = anObject;
    [self revert:self];

    /* Register for notifications from the new model. */
    [[NSNotificationCenter defaultCenter] addObserver:self
        selector:@selector(indexDidChangeAgents:)
        name:IndexDidChangeAgentsNotification
```

```
        object:model];

    return self;
}
```

Perhaps a ControlIndex will only have one model throughout its life-time, but this implementation of **setModel:** is clean—it doesn't assume anything about its usage. First **setModel:** removes the receiver as an observer of all notifications. It changes the **model**, and reverts the display. Finally, it adds itself as an observer of notifications sent by the new model. **indexDidChangeAgents:** is specified as the callback method for any action that changes the **agents** array.

Next, implement Index's **addAgent:** method to post an IndexDid-ChangeAgentNotification, as in:

```
- (void)addAgent:(Agent *)anAgent
{
    if (![agents containsObject:anObject])
        [agents addObject:anObject];
    [agents sortUsingSelector:@selector(compare:)];

    /* Notify dependents. */
    [[NSNotificationCenter defaultCenter]
        postNotificationName:IndexDidChangeAgentsNotification
        object:self];

    return;
}
```

Similarly, implement Index's **removeAgent:** method to post an Index-DidChangeAgentNotification, as in:

```
- (void)removeAgent:(Agent *)anAgent
{
    [agents removeObject:anObject];

    /* Notify dependents. */
    [[NSNotificationCenter defaultCenter]
        postNotificationName:IndexDidChangeAgentsNotification
        object:self];

    return;
}
```

Finally, ControlIndex's **indexDidChangeAgents:** method should update the interface objects accordingly, as in:

```
- (void)indexDidChangeAgents:(NSNotification *)notification
{
    [self revert:self];
    return;
}
```

Changing the Names of Agents

Changing the name of agents was covered during design, documented in Figure 5–4—*Interaction diagram for changing the name of an agent*. As we discovered in *Adding and Removing Agents from the Index*, you can simplify this design.

The difference is that changing the name of an agent not only affects ControlIndex objects but will also reorder the index's **agents** array—it's ordered alphabetically. The updated interaction diagram shown in Figure 6–17 is similar to the previous interaction diagram except that the index receives the AgentDidChangeTitleNotification not the ControlIndex. The case of updating a collaborator's title is removed from the diagram—it's addressed in *Adding and Removing Collaborators*.

Figure 6–17 Updated interaction diagram for changing the name of an agent.

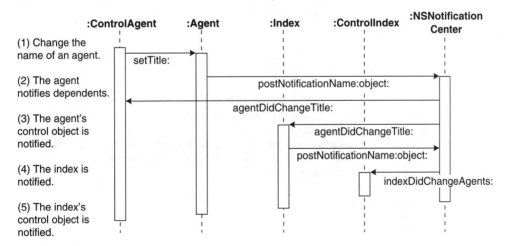

Index's **agentDidChangeTitle:** method will reorder its **agents** and post an IndexDidChangeAgentsNotification. ControlIndex objects already added themselves as observers of this notification (see *Adding and*

Removing Agents from the Index) and will update their interface objects accordingly.

Now, follow the interaction diagram shown in Figure 6–17 to implement this behavior. First, add the declarations for AgentDidChangeTitleNotification to **Agent.m** and **Agent.h**, respectively (you can paste the declarations from the **Agent.m** and **Agent.h** files contained on the enclosed disk).

The interaction diagram assumes that control objects previously added themselves as observers of AgentDidChangeTitleNotifications. Specifically, ControlAgent instances need to add themselves as observers of this notification posted by their models and any collaborators. Also, the index needs to add itself as an observer of this notification posted by each agent.

Again, the best place for a control object to add itself as an observer of notifications from its model is when the model is set. So, modify ControlAgent's **setModel:** as follows:

```
- setModel:anObject
{
    /* Unregister for notifications from agents. */
    if (model){
        [[NSNotificationCenter defaultCenter] removeObserver:self
            name:AgentDidChangeTitleNotification
            object:nil];
    }

    model = anObject;
    [self revert:self];

    /* Register for notifications from the model. */
    [[NSNotificationCenter defaultCenter]
        addObserver:self
        selector:@selector(agentDidChangeTitle:)
        name:AgentDidChangeTitleNotification
        object:model];

    return self;
}
```

Notice that the receiver is first removed as an observer of notifications posted by the old model before it's added as an observer of notifications from the new model.

Next, the index needs to add itself as an observer of AgentDidChange-TitleNotifications posted by its agents. The best place to do this is in Index's **addAgent:** method. Therefore, enhance **addAgent:** to add the receiver as an observer and **removeAgent:** to remove the receiver as an observer of the AgentDidChangeTitleNotification.

Now refer back to Figure 6–17. ControlAgent initiates the action of changing of an agent's name by sending **setTitle:** to its model when the user types in a new title. Using Interface Builder, you previously set **title**'s target to the ControlAgent instance and its action to **ok:**. Now you need to implement ControlAgent's **ok:** method to send **setTitle:** to the receiver's model, as in:

```
- (void)ok:(id)sender
{
    [model setTitle:[title stringValue]];
    [model setResponsibilities:[responsibilities string]];
    return;
}
```

Next, you enhance Agent's **setTitle:** to post an AgentDidChangeTitle-Notification, as in:

```
- (void)setTitle:(NSString *)str
{
    [title setString:str];

    /* Notify dependents. */
    [[NSNotificationCenter defaultCenter]
        postNotificationName:AgentDidChangeTitleNotification
        object:self];

    return;
}
```

Finally, you need to implement ControlAgent's and Index's callback methods. ControlAgent's **agentDidChangeTitle:** simply updates its interface objects, as in:

```
- (void)agentDidChangeTitle:(NSNotification *)notification
{
    /* The model's title changed. */
    if ([[notification object] isEqual:model]){
        [title setStringValue:[model title]];
        [window setTitle:[title stringValue]];
    }
    return;
}
```

Implement Index's **agentDidChangeTitle:** method to reorder its **agents** array, and post the IndexDidChangeAgentsNotification, as in:

```
- (void)agentDidChangeTitle:(NSNotification *)notification
{
    [agents sortUsingSelector:@selector(compare:)];

    /* Notify dependents. */
    [[NSNotificationCenter defaultCenter]
        postNotificationName:IndexDidChangeAgentsNotification
        object:self];

    return;
}
```

ControlIndex instances already added themselves as observers of an IndexDidChangeAgentsNotification and will update the display (see *Adding and Removing Agents from the Index* above). Add these methods and corresponding declarations to ControlAgent's and Index's implementation and interface files.

You can compile and test the application now. This time, when you create an agent, it appears in the index, and, when you change its title, the window's title and the entry in the index also changes.

Adding and Removing Collaborators

Not surprisingly, the implementation of adding and removing collaborators also uses the notification center. Therefore, to be concise, this section just models this behavior and summarizes the steps to complete the implementation. The user interface portion is skipped entirely (how the user actually issues an "add collaborators" command). Refer to the source code for details.

Adding and removing collaborators wasn't covered in the design chapter either, so it's helpful to first create some interaction diagrams before writing any code. This can be done without going into great detail. For the moment, assume the user can select collaborators and issue an add or remove command.

ControlAgents are the only objects that need to update the display when collaborators change. Specifically, they need to update their **table** when collaborators are added or removed, or a collaborator's name changed, causing the list to be reordered. You can simplify the design by defining one notification for all these actions—an AgentDidChangeCollaboratorsNotification posted by the ControlAgent's model.

A ControlAgent acts as the gateway between the interface objects and its model, and will eventually send **addCollaborators:** or **removeCollaborators:** to its model, passing a list of collaborators. The interaction diagram shown in Figure 6–18 traces the message flow of **addCollaborators:**. Assume the ControlAgent previously added itself as an observer of the AgentDidChangeCollaboratorsNotification and specified **agentDidChangeCollaborators:** as the callback method.

Figure 6–18 Interaction diagram for adding collaborators.

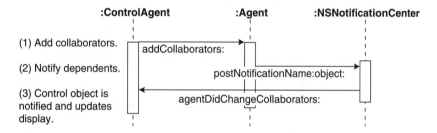

The interaction diagram for removing collaborators is identical, except that **removeCollaborators:** is sent to an agent.

At this point, you can also model the implementation of changing a collaborator's name. Assume instances of Agent added themselves as observers of AgentDidChangeTitleNotifications posted by their collaborators, and specified **agentDidChangeTitle:** as the callback method. Figure 6–19 shows the message flow of Agent's **agentDidChangeTitle:** method (refer to Figure 6–17 for the message flow before **agentDidChangeTitle:** is invoked).

Figure 6–19 Changing the name of a collaborator.

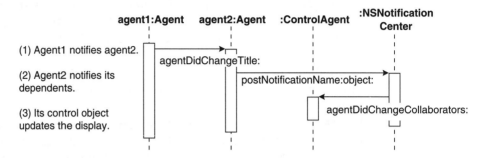

Now, step through the interaction diagrams to implement this behavior. First, add the declarations for AgentDidChangeCollaboratorsNotification to **Agent.h** and **Agent.m**. Next, Agent's **addCollaborators:** and **removeCollaborators:** methods need to post this notification as in:

```
- (void)addCollaborators:(NSArray *)anArray
{
    /* Remove objects that are already collaborators. */
    ...

    /* Add the new collaborators and sort them. */
    [collaborators addObjectsFromArray:anArray];
    [collaborators sortUsingSelector:@selector(compare:)];

    /* Register for notifications from the new collaborators */
    ...

    /* Notify dependents. */
    [[NSNotificationCenter defaultCenter] postNotificationName:
        AgentDidChangeCollaboratorsNotification object:self];

    return;
}
```

Instances of ControlAgent need to add themselves as observers of this notification, which is best done when the model is first set. Add this code to ControlAgent's **setModel:** method:

```
[[NSNotificationCenter defaultCenter]
    addObserver:self
    selector:@selector(agentDidChangeCollaborators:)
    name:AgentDidChangeCollaboratorsNotification
    object:model];
```

Implement ControlAgent's **agentDidChangeCollaborators:** method to update the display.

That takes care of adding and removing collaborators—now finish implementing the behavior of changing the name of a collaborator (follow the interaction diagram in Figure 6–19). Add some code to Agent's **addCollaborators:** method to add the receiver as an observer of Agent-DidChangeTitleNotifications as in:

```
/* Register for notifications from the new collaborators */
{
    NSEnumerator *list;
    id agent;

    list = [anObject objectEnumerator];
    while (agent = [list nextObject]) {
        [[NSNotificationCenter defaultCenter] addObserver:self
            selector:@selector(agentDidChangeTitle:) name:
            AgentDidChangeTitleNotification object:agent];
    }
}
```

Finally, implement Agent's **agentDidChangeTitle:** method to reorder its collaborators and post an AgentDidChangeCollaboratorsNotification. ControlAgent objects already added themselves as observers of this notification and will update their displays.

That part of the implementation was easy. Now you need to implement a friendly user interface for adding and removing collaborators. For example, using the Cards application on the enclosed disk, you can drag selected agents from the index and drop them on a card. This action adds collaborators to the agent represented by that card. You remove collaborators by selecting them from the card's list of collaborators and clicking the Remove button (located on the card). Implement your user interface similarly, or invent your own user interface for adding and removing collaborators.

Deleting Agents

Deleting an agent is non-trivial. If an agent is deleted, not only should its card be removed, but it should be removed from the index and any other card that has it listed as a collaborator.

When the user deletes an agent in the Cards application, you really want that object to be deallocated, not simply decrease its reference count. Therefore, sending **release** or **autorelease** to an agent is not enough; other objects, such as the index, retain it by adding it to its NSArray. So you need to implement your own **delete** method.

This behavior was covered during design and the message flow of **delete** documented in Figure 5–6—*Interaction diagram for deleting an agent.* All other objects that keep a reference to the agent must add themselves as observers of an ObjectWillDeleteNotification posted by the agent. Their callback methods should remove any references to the "deleted" agent and release it (if they retained it). Eventually, the agent's reference count reaches zero and it is deallocated. Implement this behavior by stepping through this interaction diagram.

First, implement Agent's **delete** to force a **dealloc** by notifying dependents, posting an ObjectWillDeleteNotification, as shown. Add this method and corresponding declaration to **Agent.m** and **Agent.h** respectively.

```
- (void)delete
{
    /* Notify dependents. */
    [[NSNotificationCenter defaultCenter]
        postNotificationName:ObjectWillDeleteNotification
        object:self];
    return;
}
```

ControlAgents need to add themselves as observes of their model being deleted (add this code to ControlAgent's **setModel:** method). Agents need to add themselves as observers of ObjectWillDeleteNotifications sent by their collaborators (add this code to Agent's **addCollaborators:** method). The index also needs to add themselves as observers of ObjectWillDeleteNotifications sent by its agents (add this code to Index's **addAgent:** method).

Finally, implement the **willDelete:** callback methods for ControlAgent, Agent, and Index. ControlAgent's **willDelete:** method should simply release itself and close its window (consequently releasing its window and views). Agent's **willDelete:** method should remove the deleted agent from its **collaborators** array by invoking **removeCollaborators:**. Similarly, Index's **willDelete:** method should remove the deleted agent from its **agents** array by invoking **removeAgent:**. These methods already notify control objects of changes, so interface objects will be updated accordingly.

Note, the notification center does not own observers and therefore does not retain them. However, the notification center still needs to know when an observer is about to be deallocated so it can be removed as a recipient of notification messages. Therefore, any object that observes notifications should send **removeObserver:** to the notification center just before its deallocated. Add this line of code to Agent, Index, ControlIndex, and ControlAgent's **dealloc** methods:

```
[[NSNotificationCenter defaultCenter] removeObserver:self];
```

You're not done until you create a user interface for selecting and deleting agents. The Cards application on the enclosed disk allows users to select agents from the index and click on a Delete button to permanently delete them. Here's a summary of the steps to complete the implementation (see source code for details):

❑   Implement ControlIndex's **deleteAgents:** method to open a panel confirming if the user really wants to delete the agents (use **NSRunAlertPanel()**) and if the user clicks OK, send **delete** to the selected agents.

❑   Add **deleteAgents:** to **ControlIndex.h**, open **ControlIndex.nib**, and drop **ControlIndex.h** on it to update the Classes folder.

❑   Add a Delete button to the index window.

❑   Set the Delete button's target/action to the File's Owner and **deleteAgents:** method.

Saving and Loading

Single-user applications are usually document based. There's no need to use a fancy database because the information is not shared dynamically—there's no need for concurrency control as with multi-user applications. Therefore, this section simply uses OpenStep's archiving mechanism to save and load entity objects to and from disk.

The *archiving mechanism* allows you to write and read whole object graphs to and from a file. You control what objects are archived and the mechanism ensures that each object is archived only once (often object graphs contain multiple references to the same object).

Your objects become archivable by simply adopting the NSCoding protocol. The NSCoding protocol defines only two methods: **encodeWith-Coder:** is used to write the object and **initWithCoder:** is used to read the object.

The **encodeWithCoder:** and **initWithCoder:** methods take a single argument—an instance of NSCoder. If the NSCoder object is an instance of NSArchive or NSUnarchive respectively (concrete subclasses of NSCoder), then the object is saved or loaded to and from disk. However, if the NSCoder object is an instance of NSPortCoder, then the object is copied and sent over the wire via a Distributed Object message. Therefore, you don't have to write additional code for Distributed Objects—both mechanisms use the NSCoding protocol.

Actually, you never invoke **encodeWithCoder:** or **initWithCoder:** directly—these methods are invoked by the mechanism. You archive an object by sending **archiveRootObject:toFile:** to the NSArchiver class, and unarchive an object by sending **unarchiveObjectWithFile:** to the NSUnarchiver class. For example, ControlApp's **save:** action method gets the file name from the user using an NSSavePanel and then archives the index and all its agents, as in:

```
/* Display the NSSavePanel. */
if ([savePanel runModalForDirectory:NSHomeDirectory()
        file:pathname]){
    [pathname setString:[savePanel filename]];
    if (![NSArchiver archiveRootObject:index toFile:pathname])
        NSBeep();
}
```

The **archiveRootObject:** and **unarchiveObjectWithFile:** methods automatically create instances of NSArchive and NSUnarchive for you and will eventually send the NSCoding protocol messages to your objects.

All entity objects that you want to archive need to adopt to the NSCoding protocol. NSCoder provides all the building blocks for implementing this protocol. For example, Agent's **encodeWithCoder:** method looks like:

```
- (void)encodeWithCoder:(NSCoder *)coder
{
    [coder encodeObject:collaborators];
    [coder encodeObject:responsibilities];
    [coder encodeObject:title];
    return;
}
```

The **encodeObject:** method archives an Objective-C object and recursively sends **encodeWithCoder:** to objects it references. In this example, all of Agent's instance variables are objects. However, NSCoder provides other **encode...** methods for other types of instance variables such as **encodeRect:** and **encodePropertyList:** (see NSCoder class specification for details).

Agent's **initWithCoder:** implementation is also simple:

```
- (id)initWithCoder:(NSCoder *)coder
{
    collaborators = [[coder decodeObject] retain];
    responsibilities = [[coder decodeObject] retain];
    title = [[coder decodeObject] retain];
    return self;
}
```

The **decodeObject** method reads an Objective-C object and recursively sends **initWithCoder:** to objects that it archived. Note, the objects returned by **decodeObject** must be retained because they are owned by **coder** and will be released when **coder** is released.

Your **encodeWithCoder:** and **initWithCoder:** methods must encode and decode objects in the exact same order for the mechanism to work properly. You can omit objects entirely from the archive by simply not including them in these methods.

Note, NSObject does not conform to the NSCoding protocol, but many other Foundation Kit classes do, such as NSArray and NSString. If your superclass conforms to the NSCoding protocol, you should incorporate the superclass implementations when overriding the NSCoding protocol methods. In this example, the entity objects Index and Agent all inherit from NSObject, so there are no superclass implementations to incorporate.

You may need to add additional setup code to—**initWithCoder:**. For example, Agent and Index objects need to add themselves as observers of notifications. This information, maintained by the notification center, is not part of the archive.

Now that you can archive entity objects, you need to design the user interface for saving and loading the Cards "document." This is not hard to do if you use NSSavePanel and NSOpenPanel. See the source code on the enclosed disk for details.

Testing the Application

You have completed the first cycle of development (the first iteration of analysis, design, and implementation) and now have a working version of the Cards application that implements some basic functions. Using this version of Cards, you can display the index, create agents, change agent attributes (including the name of agents), add and remove collaborators, and delete agents. You can also save and load a Cards "document" containing the index and agents you created.

If you have been programming while at the same time reading this chapter, now is the time to check in your source code. This version of Cards is functional and can be given to users either to solicit feedback or to use for demos. But before you release it, test it thoroughly and fix any remaining bugs:

❑   Run the application from within the debugger—the index should appear.

❑   Add a couple of agents by choosing New from the Cards menu.

❑   Change the name of agents, enter the responsibilities text, and add collaborators.

❑   Change the name of an agent again, and verify that all references to the agent—on all cards—are updated.

❑   Remove a collaborator and it should be removed from the collaborator table.

❑   Now delete an agent and verify that it is removed from the index and all other cards that reference it.

❑   Finally, save your Cards document, quit the application, re-run the application, and load the same document. The index should appear in the same state as before.

Figure 6–20 shows what the application might look like after creating some CRC cards:

Figure 6–20 Creating CRC cards using the Cards application.

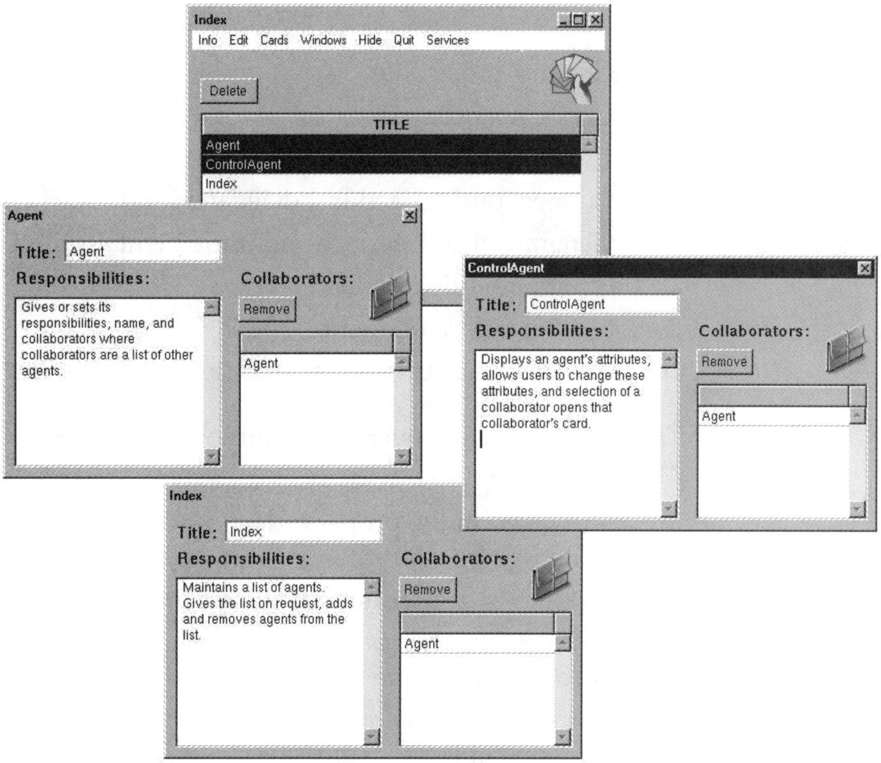

Summary

This chapter covers the first iteration of the Cards implementation that focuses on just the basic functionality (for example, creating and editing cards). It is written in tutorial-style so you can implement your own version of Cards while reading along. Only interesting aspects of the implementation are covered, such as synchronizing all the views. Refer to Appendix D—*Class Specifications* and the source code on the enclosed disk for the complete implementation. The second iteration of the implementation stage which addresses group collaboration is covered in Chapter 7—*Distributed Objects*.

This chapter also provides an introduction to using OpenStep developer tools, specifically Project Builder and Interface Builder. You learn how to:

❑   Create a project file.

❑   Create new classes.

❑   Create windows and views.

❑   Connect outlets, actions, delegates, and the File's Owner.

❑   Generate class interface and implementation files.

❑   Create module nib files.

❑   Modify the main menu.

❑   Compile and run your application.

This chapter covers several very important OpenStep mechanisms:

❑   The *initialization mechanism* ensures that all instance variables are initialized in the proper order.

❑   The *deallocation mechanism* ensures that all memory allocated by an instance is deallocated when that instance is deallocated.

❑   The *archiving mechanism* allows you to write and read whole object graphs to and from disk.

❑   The *notification center* is a mechanism for broadcasting notifications from one object to many objects.

In addition, this chapter contains examples using OpenStep classes: NSString, NSArray, NSApplication, NSTableView, NSWindow, NSButton, and NSTextField.

Distributed Objects   7

One of the motivations for writing this book is to demonstrate the power of Distributed Objects—the enabling technology that will bring your enterprise (possibly kicking and screaming) into the New Information Age.

Distributed applications mean the end of monolithic applications that hog computer resources and require large teams of developers to support. Distributed applications are small because the bulk of their work can be implemented by *services*, that is, other programs that offer a common service, such as a spelling checker or shared workspace. These applications and services can communicate via Distributed Objects. Distributed Objects is not isolated to one machine, but can send messages to processes running on different machines on local-area or wide-area networks. Services can be shared by multiple applications, and open the door for designing true groupware applications—real time exchange of information and ideas.

In addition, if you are using Portable Distributed Objects (PDO) (called DOL'E on Microsoft Windows) your applications can communicate with other applications and services running on heterogeneous systems. PDO is simply the Distributed Objects portion of OpenStep, including the Objective-C language and runtime system, Foundation Kit, Network Name Server, and some development tools, ported to other platforms such as HP-UX. PDO will even communicate with objects in other Distributed Object systems, such as OMG CORBA implementations and Microsoft's OLE/COM objects. For example, using PDO, your application could send messages to Microsoft Excel running on Microsoft Windows.

Note, Distributed Objects is not based on Remote Procedure Call (RPC) used by most client-server architecture. You need to open your minds to new possibilities when using Distributed Objects. There are no restrictions on which processes are clients and which are servers. In fact, all connections made using OpenStep's Distributed Objects system are peer-to-peer. Sending a message to a server might trigger messages from that server to other services and applications—whatever it takes to get the job done. Therefore, client-server and peer-to-peer are just roles that Distributed Objects supports.

Furthermore, Distributed Objects in OpenStep is easy to use because it's built right into the Objective-C runtime system. You do not need to write special code to send a Distributed Objects message. The Objective-C runtime system knows if the recipient of the message is remote and will distribute the message accordingly. In most cases, your classes look the same, regardless of whether or not you are using Distributed Objects. Therefore, your software is just as reusable.

However, Distributed Objects has its pitfalls. Without giving it much thought, you could easily program a rats nest of Distributed Objects messages. Services and applications may hang or crash without you knowing why. The key to successfully using Distributed Objects is to have a good design, that needs to consider where your entity objects are created and reside and how they are accessed. This is not much different from designing a single process application where you encapsulate one framework of classes from another. In the end, your design will be more modular and maintainable regardless if you use Distributed Objects or not.

There are so many applications for Distributed Objects that this chapter simply can not address them all. Instead, this chapter focuses on the most common application of Distributed Objects—implementing client-server architectures. Large enterprises often need to store their "enterprise" objects in shared databases, accessible by multiple applications. Similar to the problems faced with implementing a database server, your server applications may need to support reliable transactions that take into account concurrency (multiple client applications accessing the same server objects). Even if your application does not fit the client-server model, you will benefit from exploring the issues raised when designing client-server applications.

This chapter is organized into three parts. The first section covers the basics on how to program with Distributed Objects. The second section addresses design and high level issues when implementing client-server applications. The last section covers security issues which are very important if you plan to make your applications available to the "world."

Again, the Cards application is used to present instructive and often non-trivial examples. This chapter covers only the interesting aspects of the Cards groupware features outlined in Chapter 4—*Analysis* (refer to Appendix D—*Class Specifications* and the source on the enclosed disk for the complete implementation). The examples presented here assume familiarity with material covered in previous chapters:

❑ Chapter 4—*Analysis* covers the analysis stage of the groupware features.

❑ Chapter 5—*Design* addresses the design.

❑ Chapter 6—*Implementation* covers the implementation of the single-user version of Cards.

This chapter ties all the other chapters together. The premise is that you need more emphasis on design to implement distributed applications. Distributed applications are by nature more complex, and the analysis and design stages of development can not be skipped. The notation is invaluable in documenting the complexity of distributed systems. Interaction diagrams in particular are very handy when analyzing the behavior of Distributed Object messages.

Terminology

Even though OpenStep's Distributed Objects implementation is a peer-to-peer architecture as opposed to a strict client-server architecture, it is still convenient to use the terms client and server. Consistent with Open-Step documentation, this book uses the term *client* to refer to the object sending a Distributed Object message and *server* to refer to the remote object receiving that message. Remember, these terms are used loosely and are context sensitive. In a peer-to-peer architecture, an object can at times be a client and other times be a server. Therefore, in this context, client and server are just roles that objects play at any point in time.

However, in most designs there's still a process that plays the role of a conventional server, as in a database server. This process typically has no user interface, runs in the background, and may run on dedicated hardware if needed. This book refers to these kinds of processes as *server applications*, applications that perform some task on behalf of other applications. Other processes that use server applications to get their jobs done and typically have a user interface are called *client applications*. *Application* is used generically to refer to any OpenStep program.

The Basics

This section provides an introduction to using Distributed Objects. It covers the basics of how to vend objects, use protocols for efficiency, avoid memory leaks and dangling references, and gracefully handle errors, such as application deaths.

Vending Objects

For Distributed Objects to work, first an application must *vend* a root object—make it available to receive Distributed Object messages. It's called a *root object* because clients initially make a connection to the root object and obtain references to other remote objects by sending messages to the root object. An application can also vend an object by returning it to a client, either as a message return value or through a message argument.

You vend the root object by giving it a name and registering it with the Network Name Server as in:

```
id myConnection, session;

/* Create the root object and make it available to clients. */
session = [Session new];
myConnection = [NSConnection defaultConnection];
[myConnection setRootObject:session];
[myConnection registerName:@"session"];
```

There's a default NSConnection object per thread that uses the current NSRunLoop to service Distributed Object messages. Applications based on the Application Kit already have an NSRunLoop running to service mouse and keyboard events, as well as Distributed Object messages. Other applications need to explicitly start an NSRunLoop as in:

```
[[NSRunLoop currentRunLoop] run];
```

The root object name, "session," is later used by clients to open connections to the remote root object, as in:

```
session = [[NSConnection
    rootProxyForConnectionWithRegisteredName:"session"
    host:@"*"] retain];
```

Note, clients must know the name of a root object to make this connection. However, clients do not need to know the name of the host. If you specify "*" as the host name, as above, you will connect to any root object on the local subnet with that name. If you specify **nil** as the host name, then only the local host is searched.

You can then send messages directly to remote objects that you receive from the root object. For example, in this code fragment, the client Cards application creates a ControlIndex object by getting its model, an instance of Index, from the **session** remote object.

```
controller = [[ControlIndex new] setModel:[session index]];
```

That's all there is to creating a distributed application! Other than the initial registration of the root object and connection to the root object, the rest of the code is the same. Most important, only a few classes need contain Distributed Objects specific code—all other classes are reusable by single process applications. For example, in the Cards application, vending the root object and opening a connection to the root object are implemented by the ControlApp objects (delegates of NSApp).

How Distributed Objects Work

Let's divert for a moment to clarify what is actually happening. When you make a connection to a root object from a client, an NSConnection object is created on both the server and client side to service incoming and outgoing messages. When you send a message to a remote object, you are actually sending messages to instances of NSDistantObject, a subclass of the NSProxy root class, hereafter simply called *proxies*.

The proxy forwards messages it receives to the remote object via its NSConnection object. From the sender's point of view, the proxy behaves just like the remote object, except when you send it the **isProxy** message it will return YES; whereas objects that inherit from NSObject will return NO. You can also examine an object in the debugger to see if it's local or remote.

Now, the reason this architecture is peer-to-peer, not strictly client-server, is because the recipient of a distributed message can also send distributed messages, not only to the sender of the original message but to other remote objects located in other processes. In some cases, a process that at one moment is a server, later is a client by initiating a distributed message.

For example, Figure 7–1 illustrates the message flow of adding an agent to the index. This diagram contains an enhancement to the Booch Notation to show concurrent processes. Rectangles are used to enclose objects that reside in the same process. Note, the interface and control objects reside in client applications, whereas the entity objects reside in the server application. There are two ControlIndex objects, one for each client application (run by each participant). The ControlApp object resides in the client application that initiated the action of adding a new agent. The Session root object and other entity objects reside in the server application that represents the shared workspace.

Figure 7–1   Adding agents using the Session object.

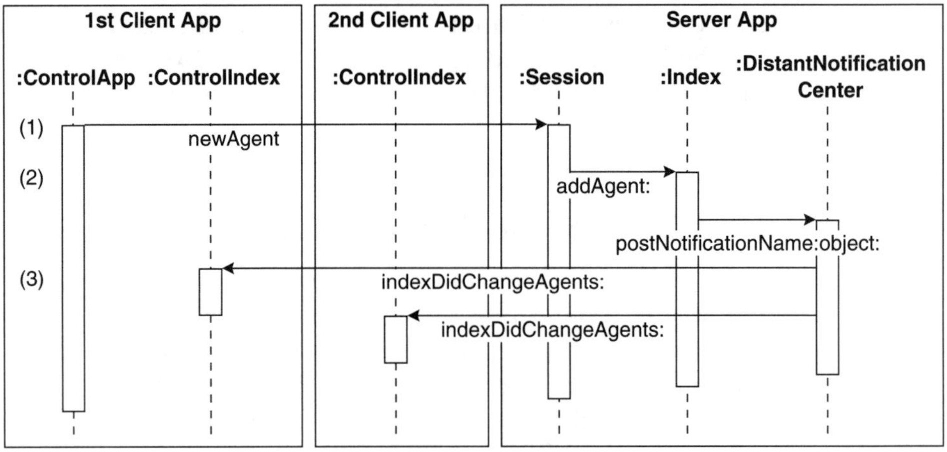

(1)   Creates an agent.

(2)   Adds an agent to the index, and posts a notification.

(3)   Control objects in different processes receive notification and update their displays.

The Session object is the recipient of the first Distributed Object message, **newAgent**. The **newAgent** method creates and adds a new Agent object to its **index**. Consequently, its **index** posts an IndexDid-ChangeAgentsNotification and the notification center sends **indexDid-ChangeAgents:** to both ControlIndex objects. These objects consequently update their displays so that all participants see the new agent appear in their views of the index.

Since the second ControlIndex object resides in another process (not the process that initiated the **newAgent** message), a new connection is opened to that process where the notification center assumes the role of the client, initiating the **indexDidChangeAgents:** message, and the ControlIndex object assumes the role of the server, processing that message.

Also, an NSConnection can receive remote messages while its already processing another. After **newAgent** is invoked, the first client application returns to the NSRunLoop waiting for the reply, and is, therefore, free to process the **indexDidChangeAgents:** message sent by the server application. If **newAgent** is instead blocked, both processes would hang or time-out, and the user action of adding an agent would fail. Basically, the default non-blocking behavior allows local and remote objects to behave as if they are in the same process. In fact, the message flow shown in Figure 7–1 is the same, regardless if Distributed Objects is used. *Designing Client-Server Applications* explores alternate configurations of the Distributed Object system.

Using Protocols

You can improve the efficiency of Distributed Object messages by using protocols. Normally, a message to a remote object makes two round-trips to the server. The first trip gets the method signature and the second trip actually sends the message. The method signature is needed to get the argument types and encode them properly before sending the message. You can eliminate the first round-trip by specifying the protocol (and therefore the method signatures) the remote object conforms to. You do this whenever you receive a vended object, as in:

```
session = [[NSConnection
    rootProxyForConnectionWithRegisteredName:"session"
    host:@"*"] retain];
[session setProtocolForProxy:@protocol(Session)];
```

Normally, you define the protocol to include only the messages you expect remote objects to send. In the Cards example, the Session protocol and class declaration are similar:

```
@protocol Session
- (BOOL)setName:(NSString *)string;
- index;
- (NSNotificationCenter *)defaultCenter;
- newAgent;
- (void)newIndex;
@end
```

Since Session is the only class that adopts this protocol, the protocol name is the same as the class name. You add the protocol name to the end of the interface declaration line to indicate that Session adopts this protocol, as in:

```
@interface Session : NSObject <Session>
...
@end
```

Refer to Appendix B—*Objective-C* for more details on using protocols.

It makes a great deal of sense to routinely define protocols for your most commonly vended objects by both clients and servers. However, it may be impractical to create a protocol for every vended object if they are numerous and diverse.

Using protocols can also reduce the software dependencies between client and server applications. For example, a server application could publish just the protocols (export only the protocol headers) to client applications and thereby control access to its implementation. However, nothing prevents a client from sending a message that isn't in the protocol (in which case, two round-trips will be made). You can use NSProtocolChecker, a NeXT extension to OpenStep, to enforce protocols (see the NSProtocolChecker class specification for details).

Avoiding Dangling References and Memory Leaks

If you already use the release mechanism in your single process program, dangling references and memory leaks rarely occur (refer to Chapter 5—*Design* for how the release mechanism works). However, there are a few instances where dangling references may appear when using Distributed Objects.

Dangling references may appear when you do not retain a vended object. Because connections own their proxies, proxies are released when their connection is released. Connections may be released at any time when they are no longer needed. Since you can not predict when this might happen, you may inadvertently send a message to an invalid proxy, which will raise an exception. So the ownership rule needs a slight addendum: only retain objects you own *unless they are remote*.

For example, even though control objects in the Cards application don't "own" their models—entity objects are not *part of* control objects—they must retain them for Distributed Objects to work. Therefore, ControlIndex and ControlAgent's **setModel:** methods must be modified to release the old model and retain the new model.

You can fix your classes easily enough; however, some OpenStep classes do not retain objects they reference—again, because they do not own them. Unfortunately, NSNotificationCenter, used heavily in the Cards design, is one of the OpenStep classes that does not retain objects—it does not retain observers. Beware, most Application Kit classes do not retain their delegate or target outlets either.

In the Cards design, control objects must add themselves as observers of notifications sent by the remote notification center, because that's where entity objects will post their notifications. This is easily implemented by adding a **defaultCenter** method to all entity objects that returns the NSNotificationCenter used by the receiver. Control objects should send **defaultCenter** to their models to get the notification center, not simply use the default notification center for their thread.

For example, Figure 7–2 traces the message flow of sending **setTitle:** to an agent—the action of one participant changing the name of an agent. Again, rectangles are used to enclose objects that reside in the same process. This message triggers several notifications. Notice that ControlAgent receives notification from a remote instance of DistantNotificationCenter, located in the server application along with the entity objects.

Figure 7–2   Changing the name of an agent using Distributed Objects.

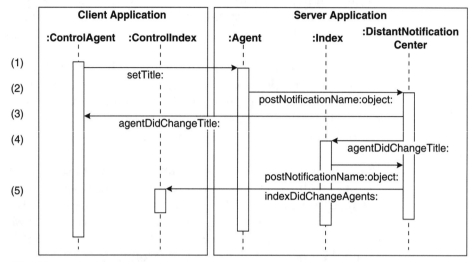

(1)   Change the name of an agent.

(2)   The agent notifies dependents.

(3)   The agent's control object is notified.

(4)   The index is notified.

(5)   The index's control object is notified.

However, since notification centers do not retain observers, proxies for control objects may be invalid when the notification center attempts to send them a notification. You can fix this by creating a subclass of NSNotificationCenter that explicitly retains and releases remote observers. In the Cards application, this class is called DistantNotificationCenter. Entity objects should implement **defaultCenter** to return an instance of this new class, not NSNotificationCenter.

DistantNotificationCenter avoids dangling reference by simply overriding the primitive methods that add and remove observers:

```
- (void)addObserver:(id)observer selector:(SEL)aSelector
            name:(NSString *)aName object:(id)anObject
{
    /* Retain distant observers. */
    if ([observer isProxy] &&
            ![observers containsObject:observer])
        [observers addObject:observer];
    return [super addObserver:observer selector:aSelector
        name:aName object:anObject];
}
```

The **observers** instance variable is an NSMutableArray containing all the remote observers. NSMutableArray retains its objects. This array comes in handy later in *Application Deaths*.

Application Deaths

Your application should observe NSConnectionDidDieNotifications posted by an NSConnection object when the remote process it was serving dies. This could happen when the user simply quits a client application, or more drastically, the machine that runs your server application crashes, leaving your client applications hanging. Therefore, you should observe this notification on both the server and client sides. Your callback methods need to clean up references to the remote objects which have become invalid.

It's easy to observe NSConnectionDidDieNotifications as follows:

```
/* Register for application deaths (from any connection). */
[[NSNotificationCenter defaultCenter] addObserver:self
    selector:@selector(connectionDidDie:)
    name:NSConnectionDidDieNotification
    object:nil];
```

If you want to observe this notification posted by a particular NSConnection object, specify that object in the **object:** argument. You can also get the NSConnection object for a specific remote object by sending **connectionForProxy** to its NSDistantObject.

It's much more difficult to implement the callback method, **connectionDidDie:**. You can obtain the NSConnection object that posted the notification by sending **object** to the NSNotification object, and obtain the proxies that belong to that connection by invoking **remoteObjects**. You could then traverse your entire object graph and remove all references to these invalid proxies, but this could be expensive or impractical. Perhaps, removing the reference is not sufficient. Perhaps related objects, such as control and interface objects, should be deleted if their entity object becomes invalid. Consequently, how you clean up invalid proxies is application-dependent.

For example, in the Cards application, on the server side, only the Distant-NotificationCenter object maintains references to remote objects—entity objects know nothing about control and interface objects that reside in client applications. Therefore, it's sufficient if the DistantNotificationCenter object adds itself as an observer of all NSConnectionDidDieNotifications. DistantNotificationCenter's **connectionDidDie:** method is invoked when any client application dies and simply removes the invalid proxies as observers of notifications.

Now, the client application is connected only to the server application—it never communicates directly to other client applications. Therefore, it's sufficient if the ControlApp object adds itself as an observer of all NSConnectionDidDieNotifications posted by the root NSConnection object. The dilemma is what do you do if a server dies?

In the Cards application, the control and interface objects are invalid if their models are invalid. It would be difficult to retry opening the connection to the root object and, if successful, reuse the existing control and interface objects. Also, the client application may become "out of sync" with the server. Perhaps the network connection with the server is down, but other client applications continued to communicate with the server and modify the entity objects. It's safer if you notify the user of the situation, delete the control and interface objects, and then wait for the server to become available again (meanwhile, the application could revert to single-user mode); or simply display a warning panel and terminate the application.

Handling Other Errors

Most other errors using Distributed Objects will raise exceptions, so you need to write exception handlers to catch them. You do this by placing the macros NS_DURING and NS_HANDLER around the application code that might raise an exception, called the *exception handling domain*. Then you place the code that handles exceptions between the NS_HANDLER and NS_ENDHANDLER macros, called the *local exception handler*, as in:

```
- (void)ok:(id)sender
{
NS_DURING
    [model setTitle:[title stringValue]];
    [model setResponsibilities:[responsibilities string]];
```

```
NS_HANDLER
    NSLog (@"%@ %s: %@", [self description], sel_getName(_cmd),
          localException);
    [localException raise];/* Re-raise the exception. */
NS_ENDHANDLER

    return;
}
```

When an exception is raised within the exception handling domain, control jumps to the local exception handler. Otherwise, the local exception handler code is not executed.

The local exception handler has access to the raised exception through a local variable called **localException**. If the local exception handler can not handle the particular exception, it can re-raise the exception by sending **raise** to **localException**. Perhaps some parent exception handler will catch it and take the appropriate action, but in most cases when using the Application Kit, control simply returns to the current NSRunLoop. For more details on exception handling, see the NSException class specification.

The local exception handler, in the code example above, simply logs what exception was raised and where it occurred. Refer to the NSConnection and NSProxy class specifications for the types of exceptions that might be raised when using Distributed Objects.

Designing Client-Server Applications

Distributed Objects give you the freedom to create any architecture you like. Multiple client and server applications can all communicate with each other directly. However, the most common architecture is the traditional *client-server architecture,* where multiple client applications make requests to server applications, not to each other. Servers typically provide the front-end to the database, and in an OO design, the server could contain all shared objects, persistent and transient. Exploring the design of client-server applications is very instructive, since it raises some important issues such as concurrency.

This section presents guidelines for designing client-server applications and several ways to configure Distributed Objects using non-trivial examples from the Cards application. It also contains an example of object locking as a solution to the concurrency problem.

Guidelines

Although an application that uses Distributed Objects may easily be converted to not using Distributed Objects (just merge client and server application code into a single application), the converse is not true. There are some basic rules of design that need to be followed when implementing client-server applications. Some of these rules are just based on good OO design principals, such as encapsulation.

Rule 1:   Shared entity objects should reside in server applications, while control and interface objects should reside in client applications.

Let's first review the design of the Cards application example. The second iteration of analysis addressed the groupware features and revealed new objects, Session, and Author (see Chapter 4—*Analysis*). Session stores information about the shared workspace such as the list of participants and the locking mode. Participants are Author objects which contain information such as the user's login, email address, and office location. Index already manages a list of cards and, therefore, it's only natural that it manage the list of authors as well, a super set of the participants. Figure 7–3 illustrates the enhanced class diagram containing these new objects and relationships (interface objects are not shown).

Figure 7–3   Cards groupware class diagram.

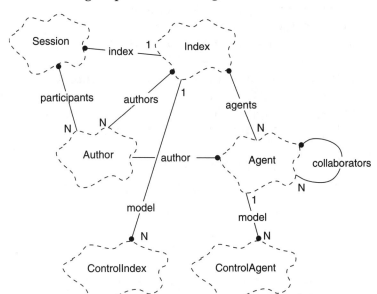

Note that in the single-process design there was only one ControlIndex object because there was only one Index object. In this design, there are multiple ControlIndex objects, one per client application, and multiple ControlAgent objects representing the same agent (indicated by the cardinality adornments placed on the target side of the class relationship).

However, this class diagram is incomplete, with respect to a distributed application, because it doesn't show which process the objects actually reside in. It's not enough to create a process diagram as in Chapter 5—*Design*. A process diagram only shows the processors and processes, not where objects reside.

Where objects reside is an important design decision, even if the decision is that some objects should "float" between processes. This information can be captured by annotating a Booch class, object or interaction diagram. Simply use a rectangle to enclose objects that reside in the same process and label the rectangle with the name of the process as shown in Figure 7–1 above and Figure 7–4 below.

Using the Jacobson Method, objects are already classified as either entity, control, or interface objects. This provides a natural boundary between server and client application objects. Entity objects are designed for maximum reuse—they have no direct references to control or interface objects, and know nothing about their types. Remember, in the Cards design, control objects add themselves as observers of entity object notifications, therefore only the notification center (on the server application side) maintains references to control objects. Conversely, control objects (on the client application side) are the only objects with references to entity objects. Interface objects only communicate with control objects. Therefore, entity objects that all client applications share should reside in the server application, and control and interface objects reside in client applications as illustrated in Figure 7–4.

Figure 7–4   Cards groupware object diagram.

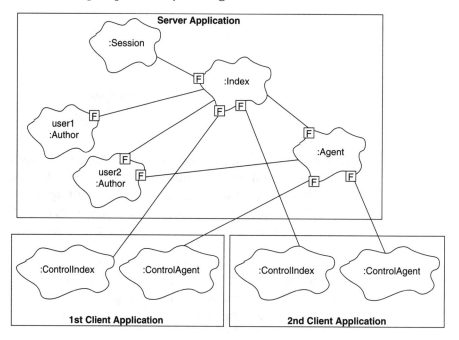

The advantage of centralizing the entity objects, which by definition represent persistent information, is that they eventually need to be stored on disk. The server application can encapsulate the mechanisms used to store these objects in a database or flat files. For example, you might want to use the Enterprise Objects Framework (EOF) to store the objects in a relational database, or simply archive the objects as shown in Chapter 6. In any case, client applications are insulated from whatever storage mechanism you choose.

Another advantage is that this design reduces the number of references to remote objects, therefore improving efficiency. It is also important that your design be understandable and therefore more maintainable. Some Distributed Object applications can be very challenging to debug.

Rule 2:   Don't publish your primary object to the world.

In the Cards application, all entity objects are accessible through the index—the index contains a list of all the cards and all the authors. However, the index does not make a good root object, because there's other information about the session, not part of the model, that client applications need to access. Also, for security reasons, it's not wise to advertise your primary object as the root object (see *Security Issues* for more details).

On the other hand, Session is the perfect root object, because it can act as the "front man" for the index. Clients will initially obtain the index from the Session object, and thereafter communicate directly with entity objects (in this way, other class relationships remain the same as in a single process application).

Rule 3:   Entity objects should be created by server applications and vended to client applications.

Once you select the root object, you can add methods to its interface that allow client applications to create entity objects shared by all.

It's easy to make a mistake, especially if you convert a single process application to use Distributed Objects. For example, in the single process Cards implementation, the ControlApp object creates an Agent object and adds it to the index as follows:

```
agent = [Agent new];
[index addAgent:agent];
```

If **index** is a remote object, then a proxy for **agent** is added to it not the actual Agent instance. Although the code will appear to work, entity objects become distributed between client applications. This causes serious problems if a user quits a client application (see *Application Deaths*).

Although OpenStep supports sending copies of objects from one process to another, in this case it's unnecessary and inefficient to do so (refer to the OpenStep reference manual for how to copy objects). Instead, the root object should provide methods that create and return entity objects on behalf of client applications. As shown in Figure 7–1, the **newAgent** method was added to Session to create and add an agent to its index. The ControlApp object that invoked **newAgent** will receive a proxy for the Agent instance. Consequently, the Session object vends a new agent to the client application.

The Need for Concurrency Control

As stated earlier, the default behavior of distributed messages is non-blocking—applications can process incoming messages while waiting for replies from outgoing messages. This non-blocking behavior allows local and remote objects to behave as if they are in the same process. The message flow shown in Figure 7–1 and Figure 7–2 would be the same for a single process program.

However, these interaction diagrams do not show what happens if the server receives conflicting requests from multiple clients. Unreliable network connections or simply lengthy processing by a client or the server can help create these situations. Figure 7–5 shows what might happen if one client initiates the action of changing an agent's title while another attempts to delete the same agent.

Suppose there's a delay when the DistantNotificationCenter object sends **agentDidChangeTitle:** to the ControlAgent object. The first client receives the message but takes a long time to process the message before it replies. While the NSConnection object is waiting for the reply it returns control to the NSRunLoop, allowing other, possibly unrelated, client requests through.

Suppose the second client application sends **delete** to the Agent object. It is attempting to remove the very same agent whose title is in the process of being changed. The server begins to process the **delete** message, but blocks when it attempts to send a notification message to the first client application. Note that the second client application also waits for a reply from the **delete** message. From the user's perspective both client applications are frozen because user input is blocked while Distributed Objects messages are not.

You can improve the responsiveness of client applications by allowing some user events through. You do this by sending **addRequestMode:** to the NSConnection object. See the NSConnection and NSRunLoop class specifications for details. Often this is done in order to display a panel allowing the user to cancel the operation if it takes too long or fails.

Figure 7–5   Multiple client requests with default non-blocking behavior.

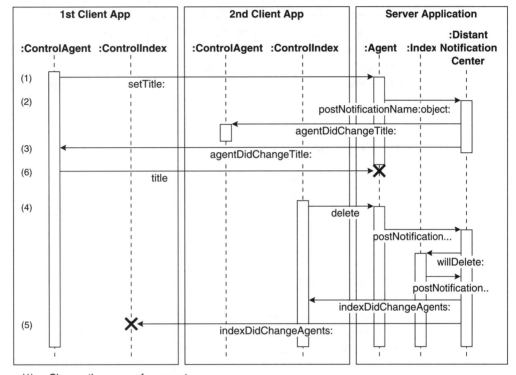

(1)   Change the name of an agent.

(2)   The agent notifies dependents.

(3)   Network goes down between 1st client and server.

(4)   2nd client removes the agent.

(5)   Messages to 1st client blocks the server until network is up.

(6)   Network is up, 1st client sends title message to released agent.

However, later, when the first client is done processing the **agentDidChangeTitle:** message, the **indexDidChangeAgents:** and consequently the **delete** messages return, allowing the second client and server applications to continue. However, when **setTitle:** finally returns to its calling context, the first client application crashes because it unknowingly sends a message to a freed object (it sends **title** to its model). The Agent object was released by the second client while the first client was in the process of changing its attributes.

This example merely illustrates the need for concurrency control when using Distributed Objects. This is no different from the problems database servers face when multiple users access the same data. There are a number of ways to configure Distributed Objects to minimize the chances of conflicts occurring. The following sections first explore different Distributed Object configurations that might solve your concurrency problems before presenting an example of object locking as a solution.

Asynchronous Messages

One way to modify the behavior of Distributed Objects is to use asynchronous messages. By default, all Distributed Object messages are *synchronous*, regardless of the return value. The client waits for the server to invoke a method, complete the processing, and send back some indication of its success, along with a return value. Even though an NSConnection can process other incoming messages while it's waiting for a reply (by returning to the NSRunLoop), it still waits for that reply.

On the other hand, *asynchronous* messages are sent without waiting for the message to be processed, so that the client can continue with the task at hand. You can make a method oneway by simply appending the **oneway** type modifier to the return value, as in:

```
- (oneway void)release;
```

Note, you can only use **oneway** for **void** return values, since if the method had another return value (such as **id** or **int**) then you would want it to be returned to the sender.

Asynchronous messages will improve the performance of both clients and servers. They also prevent the server from sending callback messages to a client before it completes some action. This way, the client has more control over when it returns control to the NSRunLoop.

In the Cards example, you can improve performance by making the callback methods **agentDidChangeTitle:** and **indexDidChangeAgents:**

asynchronous. If these messages are asynchronous, then the server application can continue the task of changing the agent's title, and only when finished returns to the NSRunLoop, awaiting new requests. There is also less chance that a second client application could remove the agent while its title is in the process of being changed.

Figure 7–6 shows a modification of the interaction diagram shown in Figure 7–2, where the notification messages are now asynchronous. The asynchronous messages are adorned with the Booch symbol for asynchronous (taken from the object diagram). The dashed rectangles were added to illustrate the old focus of control when all messages were synchronous. Although the blocks are not drawn using actual execution times, it is evident from this diagram that the performance of both the server and client applications will improve. The server application will be free sooner to process other client application requests.

Figure 7–6   Changing the name of an agent using asynchronous messages.

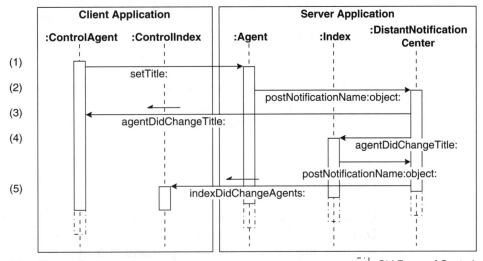

(1)   Change the name of an agent.

(2)   The agent notifies dependents.

(3)   The agent's control object is notified.

(4)   The index is notified.

(5)   The index's control object is notified.

On the other hand, it doesn't make sense for the **setTitle:** method, invoked by the client application, to be asynchronous. First of all, the client application will want to wait for a reply to ensure that the operation was successful. Also, you don't want the same user to be able to make another change before the first is completed and reflected in the user interface.

However, there are two things that can go wrong with this approach. First of all, the **agentDidChangeTitle:** and **indexDidChangeAgents:** methods make additional callbacks to their models (**agentDidChangeTitle:** gets the new title from its model to update the display). If the state of these models change while these messages are being processed, the client applications may crash in the same manner as before. It's safer if asynchronous messages do not make callbacks that depend on the sender's state. Make sure you understand the behavior of your application before you use asynchronous messages.

Secondly, client requests can slip through in a different way when using **oneway** messages. If a **oneway** message is sent to a server and the server does not acknowledge receipt of that message, then the client will return control to the NSRunLoop, waiting for that acknowledgment. *Even though a **oneway** message does not wait for a reply, it still must wait until that message is at least received by the server.* A server may not respond immediately if the network connection is down, it's overloaded, or its queue is full. Other client application requests can still slip through, just as before, creating similar problems. You may be able to fix this particular problem by setting time-outs.

Setting Time-outs

If your network connections are unreliable, you might set time-outs for Distributed Object messages. You can set the time-out value for outgoing messages and replies independently. You might take a different action if a message to a remote object times out, than if the remote object receives the message but times out waiting for a reply. In the first case, you might try again at a later time (especially if a client application initiates a request to a server application). In the second case, you might just continue execution, assuming the message to the remote object will eventually succeed (maybe its not so critical that it does), or take some other precautions assuming the message might fail.

The request time-outs apply to both synchronous and asynchronous messages. However, by definition, the reply time-out does not apply to asynchronous messages. The default time-out values are infinite. You change the defaults by sending **setRequestTimeout:** and **setReplyTimeout:** to an NSConnection object, as in:

```
[myConnection setRequestTimeout:5.0];
[myConnection setReplyTimeout:5.0];
```

The NSConnection object raises an NSPortTimeoutException when either of these time-outs are exceeded, so you need to add exception handling to your code to catch time-outs. See *Handling Other Errors* for how to write an exception handler.

Using Independent Conversation Queues

You can try a combination of synchronous and asynchronous messages and setting time-outs. But these alone are not solutions to the problem of one user action clobbering another. Cards is a typical client-server application, where messages between the client and server must be synchronous, and concurrency control is badly needed.

Distributed Objects actually has a built in feature that might solve your concurrency problems. Because an NSConnection returns control to the NSRunLoop while waiting for a reply, applications normally process arbitrary incoming messages while waiting for replies from outgoing messages. You can restrict this default non-blocking behavior by turning independent conversation queueing on. *Independent conversation queueing* only allows those messages that are part of the current conversation to be processed. Other messages, not part of the conversation, will block until the conversation ends.

You turn independent conversation queueing on by sending **setIndependentConversationQueueing:** to the NSConnection object on either the client or server side as in:

```
[myConnection setIndependentConversationQueueing:YES];
```

The resulting behavior is best illustrated by an example from the Cards application (refer to Figure 7–5). If independent conversation queueing is turned on, the conversation begins when the server application receives the **setTitle:** message. Consequently, all three applications go into a mode where they will only process messages that are part of this conversation. The conversation ends when **setTitle:** returns. Therefore, it's not possible for the second client to initiate the **delete** message while **setTitle:** is being processed.

In fact, unless you use **addRequestMode:** to allow the processing of user events, the client applications appear to block until the conversation ends. As long as requests are processed quickly, this is reasonable behavior for applications that need to be tightly synchronized. Otherwise, you could set time-outs to avoid long delays in client applications.

Note, you still can't make the notification messages in this example asynchronous. If **agentDidChangeTitle:** is asynchronous, the conversation might end (**setTitle:** might return) before **agentDidChangeTitle:** is finished processing, possibly causing the client to be "out of sync" with the server again.

Independent conversation queueing works well if the messages that begin conversations represent entire transactions. However, problems can result if a client application sends several messages to a server within the same calling context as in this implementation of ControlAgent's **ok:** method:

```
-  (void)ok:(id)sender
{
    [model setTitle:[title stringValue]];
    [model setResponsibilities:[responsibilities string]];

    return;
}
```

It's possible for the server application to process a **delete** message from a second client after **setTitle:** returns and before **setResponsibilities:** is invoked. In this case, invoking **setResponsibilities:** will fail because **model** no longer exists on the server. This is true for methods that both set and get attributes from server objects. If you can't program around this problem, a better solution is to implement some form of concurrency control.

Object Locking

If independent conversation queues don't solve your concurrency problems, then you might want to implement object locking. You can design your application to lock objects before performing some user action. You might want to implement object locking to prevent users from initiating actions that may conflict with on-going actions. For example, users might explicitly lock cards before editing, consequently disabling other users' views of that card. Object locking is not a feature directly supported by Distributed Objects—you implement this based on your own application needs.

Note, even if you use a database management system (DBMS) to store your persistent objects (for example, you use EOF to store your objects in an Informix database), you may still need object locking. The concurrency control provided by most DBMS is insufficient for OO systems. Locking tables and records in a relational database doesn't directly correspond to single or even multiple objects. Locking segments or pages in an OODBMS also does not correspond to any objects. Furthermore, your object locking mechanism can also accommodate non-persistent objects, called *transient objects*.

For example, Agent provides the following methods for locking instances:

- (BOOL)readLock;
- (BOOL)readUnlock;
- (BOOL)writeLock;
- (BOOL)writeUnlock;

Each method returns YES if the operation succeeded and NO otherwise. Multiple read locks are allowed, but all other combinations are not allowed. For example, **writeLock** returns NO if the receiver is locked for either reading or writing.

These methods are not difficult to write. Agent defines two new instance variables: **readLock** is an integer that maintains the current number of read locks, and **writeLock** is a BOOL set to YES if a write lock is active. The **readLock** method simply checks to see if there's a write lock active, and, if so, returns NO, otherwise it returns YES. If successful, **readLock** increments the count and **readUnlock** decrements the count, as in:

```
- (BOOL)readLock
{
    if (writeLock)
        return NO;
    readLock++;
    return YES;
}
```

```
- (BOOL)readUnlock
{
    if (writeLock || !readLock)
        return NO;
    readLock--;
    return YES;
}
```

The **writeLock** and **writeUnlock** methods are also easy to write as in:

```
- (BOOL)writeLock
{
    if (readLock || writeLock)
        return NO;
    writeLock = YES;
    return YES;
}

- (BOOL)writeUnlock
{
    if (readLock || !writeLock)
        return NO;
    writeLock = NO;
    return YES;
}
```

Now we can fix ControlAgent's **ok:** method to lock the Agent object before changing it, as in:

```
- (void)ok:(id)sender
{
    if ([model writeLock]){
        [model setTitle:[title stringValue]];
        [model setResponsibilities:[responsibilities string]];
        [model writeUnlock];
    }

    return;
}
```

You might want to notify the user when an operation like this fails, or better yet, augment Agent's locking methods to post notifications. ControlAgent objects can receive these notifications and disable the corresponding user interface, so that other users can not initiate actions that will conflict.

Typically, you only need to lock around user actions. In OpenStep, you would routinely lock and unlock inside action methods like ControlAgent's **ok:** and **open:** methods invoked by views.

This example of object locking may work for simple objects like Agent, but it's not a general purpose locking mechanism. Here are just some of the deficiencies:

❏   You need to decide what it means to lock an object in your application. If you lock an object, should it recursively lock all objects it owns? The implementation presented here locks only the receiver.

❏   The implementation does not support nested read or write locks, so you need to be careful where you invoke these methods in your code.

❏   The implementation does not take into account application deaths. If a client application locks an entity object and dies before it releases that lock, then other client applications will be denied access to that object. Additional bookkeeping is needed to release these locks. See *Application Deaths* for details on how to detect client application deaths.

A better approach might be to design a control object that manages locks for other objects. The archiving mechanism could be used as a model for designing such a locking mechanism. That is, the locking mechanism might define a protocol similar to NSCoding that allows an object to specify which of its components should be locked when it is locked. The control object, similar to NSArchiver, implements the actual locking methods so that they are reusable by all other objects. Unfortunately, implementing this mechanism is beyond the scope of this book.

Security Issues

You can't assume your applications are running in a friendly environment, especially if you plan to make your applications available to the world and they contain sensitive information. You should take some precautions against unauthorized access to your objects and tampering. This section covers some steps you can take to make your applications more secure.

Accessing the Root Object

First of all, you should select your root object carefully—that is, the object that is published to the world. The interface to this object should be minimal, and sensitive methods should be private. You can also use NSProtocolChecker to restrict remote access to this object and other vended objects (NSProtocolChecker is a NeXT extension to OpenStep, see the class specification for details).

It's true that client applications need to know the name of the root object to open a connection, but that name is simply a text string and there's no encryption support. It's even remotely possible that some hacker might get access to the Network Name Server entries. Remember the name is only as secure as the permissions of the operating system, so try to make the name as private as possible.

In the Cards application, users agree on a "password" prior to opening a session. This password is used to set the name of the root object. You can change the name of the root object anytime by sending **registerName:** to its NSConnection object. Connections that are already open are still valid, but changing the name prevents new connections from being opened using the old name. This strategy will at least prevent other users from joining in on your groupware session and inadvertently changing your objects—adequate security in a friendly office environment.

However, even if you implement additional verification mechanisms before vending the root object, this approach is not fool proof. Another process could still get access to your objects indirectly through a legitimate client application. Your application is only as secure as all the applications you vend your root object to.

Authentication

Currently, the best form of security is to use the authentication mechanism which is another extension to OpenStep (it may not be available on all platforms). The authentication mechanism simply allows an NSConnection object's delegate to authenticate or verify incoming and outgoing messages. How you implement the actual authentication is application-dependent. This mechanism simply provides the hooks for you to authenticate messages.

Before outgoing messages are sent, **authenticationDataForCompo-nents:** is sent to the delegate. The delegate implements this method to return its authentication stamp. The authentication stamp, an instance of NSData, is passed along with the message to the server.

Before the incoming message is processed on the server side, the delegate of its NSConnection object is sent **authenticateComponents:with-Data:**. The delegate implements this method to return YES if the incoming message passes its authentication test, otherwise NO.

You can be as creative as you like in implementing the authentication test. In the Cards example, an NSString is simply encoded by the sender and decoded by the receiver, as in:

```
static NSString *STAMP = @"s%#%*";

- (BOOL)authenticateComponents:(NSArray *)components
        withData:(NSData *)authenticationData
{
    NSString *tempString =
        [[NSString alloc] initWithData:authenticationData
                              encoding:NSUnicodeStringEncoding];

    return ([tempString isEqual:STAMP] ? YES : NO);
}

- (NSData *)authenticationDataForComponents:(NSArray *)components
{
    return [STAMP dataUsingEncoding:NSUnicodeStringEncoding];
}
```

You only need to set the delegate of the root object's connection because all child connections will be assigned the same delegate. Also, once this mechanism is setup, all messages will be authenticated, including clients that invoke **rootProxyForConnectionWithRegisteredName:**. Invoking this method will fail if the delegate for the root NSConnection is not set first. Therefore, when using authentication, clients must get the root NSConnection object first, then set its delegate, and finally get the proxy for the root object as in:

```
theConnection = [NSConnection connectionWithRegisteredName:
    "session" host:@"*"];
[theConnection setDelegate:self];
session = [[theConnection rootProxy] retain];
```

Also, expect a performance hit when using the authentication mechanism. Not only are additional messages being invoked on both the server and client, but additional data is being sent across the wire for every Distributed Object message.

Exercise

The Cards program is not a complete example of a new information age application unless it interacts with other applications and services. Such a service might be a Glossary that manages your application domain-specific terms. Some application domains have established terminology such as the video editing industry. Nevertheless, these terms need to be documented because they are often obtuse and unfamiliar to software developers. In other cases, you might need to invent new terms to convey new ideas. These terms are not necessarily agents and, therefore, don't correspond to a CRC card, but they might be used to describe an agents responsibilities. Therefore, the Cards user will want to click on unfamiliar terms in the description to display their definitions. A companion Glossary application could provide such as service to the Cards application.

Summary

Distributed Objects is the enabling technology that allows you to implement true hypermedia and groupware applications. However, programming with Distributed Objects can be tricky. You need to carefully design your distributed applications and understand your architectural requirements.

At a programming level, you need to understand how Distributed Objects works. Recipients of distributed messages can also send distributed messages, not only to the sender of the original message but other remote objects located in other processes. Servers can also process other, sometimes unrelated, distributed messages while waiting for replies from outgoing messages.

You can also use protocols to improve the efficiency of distributed messages. You need to worry about introducing dangling references and memory leaks because objects reside in different processes, and application deaths that may invalidate references to remote objects.

Distributed Objects is not limited to implementing just client-server applications—it's really a peer-to-peer architecture with many possible uses. However, Distributed Objects will most commonly be used to implement client-server applications, especially in large enterprises with shared databases. Exploring the implementation of client-server applications is also advantageous because it reveals many requirements, such as concurrency control, that might be relevant to other architectures.

There are some rules to help you design client-server applications. Shared entity objects reside in server applications, and control and interface objects reside in client applications. Entity objects are created by server applications and vended to client applications, not distributed between client applications. The root object vended by servers should also be selected with care.

The default non-blocking behavior of Distributed Objects is often not suitable for client-server applications. There are several ways to alter this behavior, such as using some asynchronous messages. Asynchronous messages are sent without waiting for a reply and therefore can improve the performance of both the client and server applications. However, in a client-server architecture, asynchronous messages sent to client applications should not make callbacks to the server application, otherwise they might conflict with other client application requests. Make sure you understand the behavior of your application before using asynchronous messages.

You can also set time-outs for sending outgoing messages and replies independently. Time-outs can sometimes avoid deadlocks or long delays due to network connectivity or programming errors.

Independent conversation queues can sometimes fix your concurrency problems. Independent conversation queueing only allows those messages that are part of the current conversation to be processed. Other messages not part of the conversation will block until the conversation ends. However, this only works well if a single message sent by a client represents an entire transaction. Otherwise, other client messages can slip through again, rendering the server objects inconsistent.

You can implement object locking above the Distributed Object system as a form of concurrency control for client-server applications. You might need to do this even if your server is a front-end to a database that supports concurrency control. The database may not be able to lock individual objects; also, your locking mechanism can be used by persistent as well as transient objects.

If you plan to export your applications to the world, then you also need to worry about security—unauthorized access to your objects and tampering. You can take some steps to limit access to your root object and its methods. However, the best approach is to use the authentication mechanism (unfortunately this is not part of the OpenStep specification, and therefore may not be available on all platforms). The authentication mechanism allows recipients to "authenticate" incoming messages before they are delivered. This mechanism allows you to be very creative on how you authenticate messages.

A Laboratory For Teaching OO Thinking[†] A

It is difficult to introduce both novice and experienced procedural programmers to the anthropomorphic perspective necessary for object-oriented design. We introduce CRC cards, which characterize objects by class name, responsibilities, and collaborators, as a way of giving learners a direct experience of objects. We have found this approach successful in teaching novice programmers the concepts of objects, and in introducing experienced programmers to complicated existing designs.

1. Problem

The most difficult problem in teaching object-oriented programming is getting the learner to give up the global knowledge of control that is possible with procedural programs, and rely on the local knowledge of objects to accomplish their tasks. Novice designs are littered with regressions to global thinking: gratuitous global variables, unnecessary pointers, and inappropriate reliance on the implementation of other objects.

Because learning about objects requires such a shift in overall approach, teaching objects reduces to teaching the design of objects. We focus on design whether we are teaching basic concepts to novices or the subtleties of a complicated design to experienced object programmers.

Rather than try to make object design as much like procedural design as possible, we have found that the most effective way of teaching the idiomatic way of thinking with objects is to immerse the learner in the "object-ness" of the material. To do this we must remove as much familiar material as possible, expecting that details such as syntax and programming environment operation will be picked up quickly enough once the fundamentals have been thoroughly understood.

---

† This article appeared in *OOPSLA '89 Conference Proceedings*. The article is by Kent Beck (Apple Computer, Inc.) and Ward Cunningham (Wyatt Software Services, Inc.) and is copyright © 1989 by the Association for Computing Machinery. Reprinted by permission.

It is in this context that we will describe our perspective on object design, its concrete manifestation, CRC (for Class, Responsibility, and Collaboration) cards, and our experience using these cards to teach both the fundamentals and subtleties of thinking with objects.

2. Perspective

Procedural designs can be characterized at an abstract level as having processes, data flows, and data stores [1], regardless of implementation language or operating environment. We wished to come up with a similar set of fundamental principles for object designs. We settled on three dimensions which identify the role of an object in design: class name, responsibilities, and collaborators.

The class name of an object creates a vocabulary for discussing a design. Indeed, many people have remarked that object design has more in common with language design than with procedural program design. We urge learners (and spend considerable time ourselves while designing) to find just the right set of words to describe our objects, a set that is internally consistent and evocative in the context of the larger design environment.

Responsibilities identify problems to be solved. The solution will exist in many versions and refinements. A responsibility serves as a handle for discussing potential solutions. The responsibilities of an object are expressed by a handful of short verb phrases, each containing an active verb. The more that can be expressed by these phrases, the more powerful and concise the design. Again, searching for just the right words is a valuable use of time while designing.

One of the distinguishing features of object design is that no object is an island. All objects stand in relationship to others, on whom they rely for services and control. The last dimension we use in characterizing object designs is the collaborators of an object. We name as collaborators objects which will send or be sent messages in the course of satisfying responsibilities. Collaboration is not necessarily a symmetric relation. For example in Smalltalk 80 [2], View and Controller operate as near equals (see example below) while OrderedCollection offers a service with little regard or even awareness of its client.

Throughout this paper we deliberately blur the distinction between classes and instances. This informality is not as confusing as it might seem because the concreteness of our method substitutes for naming of instances. This also makes our method of teaching independent of whether a class or prototype-based language is used.

3. CRC Cards

The second author invented CRC cards in response to a need to document collaborative design decisions. The cards started as a Hypercard [3] stack which provided automatic indexing to collaborators, but were moved to their current form to address problems of portability and system independence.

Like our earlier work in documenting the collaboration of objects [4], CRC cards explicitly represent multiple objects simultaneously. However, rather than simply tracing the details of collaboration in the form of message sending, CR cards place the designer's focus on the motivation for collaboration by representing (potentially) many messages as a phrase of English text.

As we currently use them, all the information for an object is written on a 4″ × 6″ index card. These have the advantage that they are cheap, portable, readily available, and familiar. Figure A-1 shows an idealized card. The class name appears underlined in the upper-left hand corner, a bullet list of responsibilities appears under it in the left two-thirds of the card, and the list of collaborators appears in the right third.

Figure A–1   A Class-Responsibility-Collaborator (CRC) index card.

Figure A-2 shows an example taken from the Smalltalk-80 image, the much-misunderstood model-view-controller user interface framework We have deliberately shown only a portion of the responsibilities each of these objects assumes for clarity of exposition. Note that the cards are placed such that View and Controller are overlapping (implying close collaboration) and placed above Model (implying supervision.) We find these and other informal groupings aid in comprehending a design. Parts, for example, are often arranged below the whole. Likewise, refinements of an abstraction can be collected and handled as a single pile of cards with the most abstract card on top where it can represent the rest.

The ability to quickly organize and spatially address index cards proves most valuable when a design is incomplete or poorly understood. We have watched designers repeatedly refer to a card they intended to write by pointing to where they will put it when completed.

Figure A–2   CRC-cards describing the responsibilities and collaborations of Smalltalk's Model, View, and Controller.

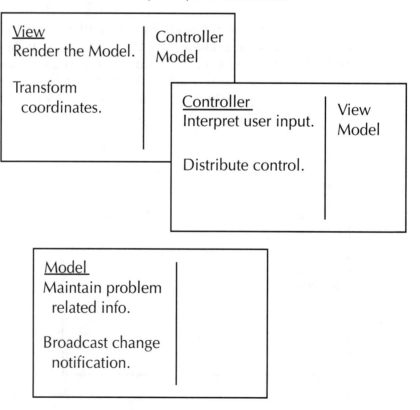

Design with the cards tends to progress from knowns to unknowns, as opposed to top–down or bottom–up. We have observed two teams arriving at essentially the same design through nearly opposite sequences, one starting with device drivers, the other with high-level models. The problem demanded a certain set of capabilities which both teams discovered in the course of fulfilling the requirements of the design.

We suggest driving a design toward completion with the aid of execution scenarios. We start with only one or two obvious cards and start playing "what-if." If the situation calls for responsibility not already covered by one of the objects, we either add the responsibility to one of the objects, or create a new object to address that responsibility. If one of the objects becomes too cluttered during this process, we copy the information on its card to a new card, searching for more concise and powerful ways of saying what the object does. If it is not possible to shrink the information further, but the object is still too complex, we create a new object to assume some of the responsibilities.

We encourage learners to pick up the card whose role they are assuming while "executing" a scenario. It is not unusual to see a designer with a card in each hand, waving them about, making a strong identification with the objects while describing their collaboration.

We stress the importance of creating objects not to meet mythical future needs, but only under the demands of the moment. This ensures that a design contains only as much information as the designer has directly experienced and avoids premature complexity. Working in teams helps here because a concerned designer can influence team members by suggesting scenarios aimed specifically at suspected weaknesses or omissions.

4. Experience

One of the contexts in which we have used CRC cards is a three-hour class entitled "Thinking with Objects," which is intended for computing professionals who have programmed, but whose jobs do not necessarily involve programming every day. The class proceeds by introducing a data flow example (a school, with the processes for teaching and administration) which is then recast in terms of objects with responsibilities and collaborators (such as Teacher, Janitor, and Principal). The class then pairs off and spends an hour designing the objects in an automatic banking machine, an exercise chosen because of everyone's familiarity with the application and its ready breakdown into objects to control the devices, communicate with the central bank database, and control the user interface. (See the appendix for a sample solution.) The exercise is followed by a definition of the terms "class," "instance," "method," and "message," and the class concludes with a brief discussion of the history and features of a variety of object-oriented programming languages.

In teaching over a hundred students this course, we have encountered no one who was unable to complete the exercise unaided, although one pair in each class usually needs a few hints to get started. Although we have done no follow-up studies, the class is considered a valuable resource in the company and is still well attended with a long waiting list almost a year after its inception.

We have also asked skilled object programmers to try using CRC cards. Our personal experience suggests a role for cards in software engineering, though we cannot yet claim a complete methodology (others [5], [6] have more fully developed methodologies that can take advantage of CRC methods). We know of one case where finished cards were delivered to a client as (partial) design documentation. Although the team that produced the cards was quite happy with the design, the recipient was unable to make sense of the cards out of context.

Another experiment illustrates the importance of the context established by the handling and discussing of cards. We had videotaped experienced designers working out a problem similar to the bank machine. Our camera placement made cards and the designers' hands visible but not the writing on the cards. Viewers of the tape had no trouble following the development and often asked that the tape be stopped so that they could express their opinions. The most telling moments came when a viewer's explanation required that he point to a blurry card in the frozen image on screen.

Finally, we have used CRC cards to advantage in explaining complex designs. A few minutes of introduction is sufficient to prepare an audience for a card based presentation. Cards can be made out in advance or written on the spot. The latter allows the complexity in a design to be revealed slowly, a process related to Dave Thomas' "lie management." The cards are being used as props to aid the telling of a story of computation. The cards allow its telling without recourse to programming language syntax or idiom.

5. Conclusion

Taking our perspective as a base, we give novices and experienced programmers a learning experience which teaches them something valuable about objects. CRC cards give the learner who has never encountered objects a physical understanding of object-ness, and prepares them to understand the vocabulary and details of particular languages. CRC cards also give useful and convincing experience with objects to those who has learned the mechanisms of objects but do not yet see their value.

Ragu Raghavan [7] has said that in the switch to objects, strong programmers become stronger, but weaker programmers are left behind. Using the cards in group settings, we found that even weaker programmers, without a deep understanding of objects, could contribute to object designs. We speculate that because the designs are so much more concrete, and the logical relationship between objects explicit, it is easier to understand, evaluate, and modify a design.

We are surprised at the value of physically moving cards around. When learners pick up an object they seem to more readily identify with it, and are prepared to deal with the remainder of the design from its perspective. It is the value of this physical interaction that has led us to resist a computerization of the cards.

It is just this problem—integrating the cards with larger design methodologies and with particular language environments—that we feel holds the most promise for the future. The need to retain the value of physical interaction points to the need for a new kind of user interface and programming environment as far beyond what we have today as our current systems are beyond the tool-oriented environments of the past.

References

[1] DeMarco, T.: Structured Analysis and System Specification, Yourdon, 1978.

[2] Smalltalk-80 image, Xerox Corp., 1983.

[3] Hypercard manual, Apple Computer, Inc.

[4] Cunningham, W. and Beck, K.: "A Diagram for Object-Oriented Programs," in Proceedings of OOPSLA-86, October 1986.

[5] Wirfs-Brock, R. and Wilkerson, B. "Object-Oriented Design: a Responsibility-Driven Approach," submitted to OOPSLA '89.

[6] Reenskaug, T.: "A Methodology for the Design and Description of Complex, Object-Oriented Systems," technical report, Center for Industrial Research, Oslo, Norway, November, 1988.

[7] Raghavan, R.: "Panel: Experiences with Reusability," in the Proceedings of OOPSLA '88, October, 1988.

Appendix

Here we provide a sample solution to the banking machine problem discussed in section 4.

Account and Transaction provide the banking model. Note that Transaction assumes an active role while money is being dispensed and a passive role thereafter.

Account	Transaction
Keeps balance and traffic.	Remote DB

Transaction	CardReader
Validate & perform money transfer.	Dispenser
	Remote DB
	Action
Keep audit info.	Account

Transactions meet their responsibilities with the aid of several objects that serve as device drivers. The Dispenser object, for example, ultimately operates the dispensing device.

The CardReader object reads and decodes the information on the bank card's magnetic strip. A common mistake would be to itemize all the information stored on the bank card. Card encoding formats must certainly be well thought out and documented. However, for the purpose of designing the objects, we need only identify where that knowledge will be placed in the program.

The RemoteDataBase drives the communication lines and interprets data transmitted across them. It creates Account objects and consumes Transaction objects.

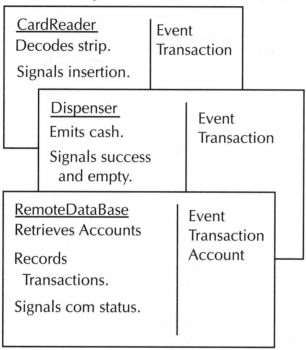

The device drivers signal exceptional or asynchronous events by adding Event objects to a shared queue.

Events drive the human interface by triggering Actions that sequence through screens. The actual format and sequence of screens will be determined by the user-interface design and will probably vary from bank to bank. We offer objects from which state–machine like interfaces can be built.

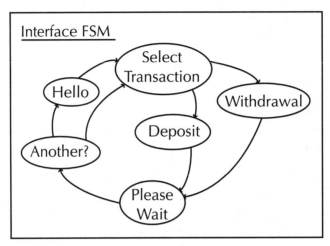

Screen objects correspond to the states and Action objects correspond to the transitions. Screens may vary in how they dispatch Actions. Actions themselves will vary in how they process events. Actions ultimately construct Transactions to which they delegate the further operating of the bank machine.

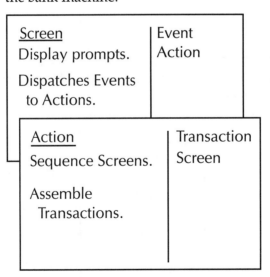

Objective-C   B

This appendix introduces the Objective-C language and presents it in terms of how the language works. The premise is that you will learn Objective-C faster, enjoy it more, and create applications with greater functionality if you have a deeper understanding of the language concepts.

Objective-C is a hybrid object-oriented programming language that supports class definitions and messaging by adding Smalltalk-like syntax extensions to the ANSI C or C++ language definitions. You select the base language with a compiler flag.

Objective-C is unique because it is one of very few C-hybrid languages that is class-oriented as opposed to type-oriented. Objective-C fully supports dynamic binding of messages to methods and classes as factory objects. This is the primary reason why Objective-C was selected to implement OpenStep.

Tools like Interface Builder that can modify user interface files without recompiling code and load custom palettes would not be possible without dynamic binding. Interface Builder is a good model for the types of applications you can build using Objective-C, and probably is one of the reasons you selected OpenStep. Therefore, this appendix focuses on the dynamic aspects of Objective-C.

The dynamics of the language also dictate a different style of programming. Smalltalk programmers will adapt easily to Objective-C, but C++ programmers that rely heavily on static typing and compile time type checking will need to shift paradigms when programming in Objective-C. Certainly, you can use the static typing features of Objective-C to mimic C++. However, in most cases, Objective-C's ability to make runtime decisions adds greater functionality to your applications.

It helps to know the base language, C or C++, before learning Objective-C, but it's not a prerequisite. Objective-C contains relatively few additions to the language, making it easy to learn. Because there's a wealth of existing OpenStep classes, you can actually learn Objective-C first and the base language on an as-needed basis. However, you will need to know the base language when implementing your own custom classes.

Objective-C is easier to learn if you understand how messaging works.

Message Syntax

The Objective-C message syntax is simple. The name of the receiving object precedes the name of the message and is surrounded by brackets:

```
[<object> <message>];
```

If the message has arguments, they appear after a ":" as in:

```
[anArray insertObject:anObject atIndex:x];
```

The object that receives the message is called the *receiver* and the object that sends the message is called the *sender*.

Message Names

In Objective-C, message names are not just used for documentation, but can be used in code to refer to messages. The ":" and argument labels are also part of the message name. In the example above, the message **insertObject:atIndex:** was sent to the object anArray. Labels describing each argument are optional when creating names (for example, the **atIndex** could have been omitted) but using descriptive labels is an Objective-C convention because it considerably improves the legibility of the code. Notice that the code fragment above reads like an English sentence: "anArray insert object, anObject, at index, x."

Dynamic Binding

What is the significance of message names and why would you want to refer to a message in Objective-C code? To answer this question, it helps to first understand how messaging works in Objective-C.

In simple terms, the Objective-C runtime system takes a receiver/message pair and (1) identifies which class the receiver belongs to, (2) finds that class's corresponding method implementation, and then (3) executes that method. Remember, a *message* tells an object what to do, not how to do it, and a *method* implements the "how" for a particular class. This approach to message passing is called *dynamic binding*, because the method is not selected until runtime. Note that this approach requires that the class structure be available at runtime for inspection.

Conceptually, a class is just a template for creating object instances that have the same data (instance variables) and methods that operate on that data. Necessarily, object instances have a private portion, the actual data values for its instance variables; and a shared portion, the class template containing a list of its methods and a reference to its superclass. For example, Figure B–1 depicts a class structure where MyClass inherits from MySuperClass which in turn inherits from NSObject.

Figure B–1   Class structure.

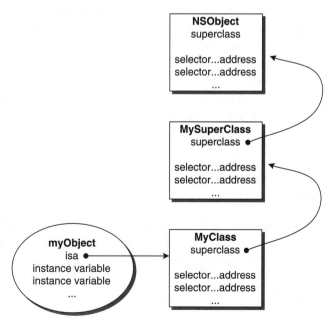

In Objective-C, each instance (the oval in Figure B–1) inherits an **isa** instance variable from the root class NSObject that points to its class object (the rectangles in Figure B–1). Through the **isa** pointer, Objective-C objects know which class they belong to, which classes they inherit from, and which messages they respond to.

For example, your program can ask an object if it responds to a message before sending it that message using **respondsToSelector:**, as in:

```
if ([anObject respondsToSelector:
      @selector(insertObject:atIndex:))
   [anObject insertObject:thisObject atIndex:index];
```

The **isa** pointer is also necessary for finding the appropriate method. Basically, the class structure includes a table mapping selectors to methods. A *selector* is an encryption of the method name, its argument types, and its return value. It's called a *selector* because it is used to *select* the appropriate method depending on the receiver. In the code example above, **@selector** is a compiler directive that lets Objective-C source code refer directly to this selector. Methods with the same name will be assigned the same selector by the compiler, so it is important to keep the argument types and return value the same as well.

The runtime system finds a method by first checking to see if the class for the object has an implementation for that selector, and then traces up the class structure, moving from descendent to ancestor, until it finds an implementation (refer again to Figure B–1). Since subclasses are checked first, subclasses can override superclass methods. Once the method implementation is found, it is placed in a hash table for easy access the next time it is called. Therefore, the first time a specific message is sent to a specific object, processing that message may take twice as long as a function call; but the second time it is much faster.

Object Types

Since a message is bound to a method at runtime, as opposed to compile time, you don't need to specify what class an object belongs to as you would in C++. You simply declare the object as an **id**, a generic data type for objects, as in:

```
id anObject;
```

Internally **id** is just a C pointer to an object structure (most Objective-C objects are dynamically allocated).

Runtime Errors

Variables declared as **id** can be set to any type of object at runtime. Therefore, it is possible to send a message to an object that doesn't have a corresponding implementation ("it can not respond to"). This type of error can not be caught at compile time, so when it occurs, the program may crash unless you take precautions.

Precautions are only necessary when you expect the object type to be unknown or one of several types, for example, if an object is being returned from a remote message call when using Distributed Objects. Using **respondsToSelector:** as in the above code example, is just one way to avoid these kinds of runtime errors. However, using *protocols*, described later, is a better way of handling disparate class types.

The advantage of dynamic binding is that your code can send messages to objects that have not even been invented yet. This allows you to build mechanisms that others can extend by simply agreeing on some common messages, and in some cases, allowing the user to enter in the messages that will be sent those "unknown" objects.

This is exactly how Interface Builder works. You can make connections between interface objects, such as buttons and text fields, supplied by OpenStep and enter in the messages those objects send to your application objects. Other user interface tools have to generate code that is compiled into your application, but Interface Builder can store the user interface layout and callbacks as objects in a file that is read at runtime. Again, Interface Builder is a good model for the types of applications you can build using Objective-C.

Self and Super

Now that you understand how message passing works, suddenly everything else about the language syntax makes sense. For instance, when you send a message to **self** and **super** within a method implementation, you are actually telling the runtime system where in the class hierarchy to begin searching for a method. **self** searches in the normal way starting with the class of the receiving object, but **super** starts the search with the superclass. Actually, with a combination of class methods and runtime functions, you can specifically request *any* superclass method implementation (although you will rarely do so).

Typically, **super** is used when overriding a method and you need to incorporate the inherited version, as in:

```
- init
{
    [super init];
    stuff = [[NSMutableArray array] retain];
    return self;
}
```

Note that **super** can only appear as the receiver in a message expression, whereas **self** is really a variable referring to the receiver in a method implementation (it is actually one of the hidden arguments to every method) and therefore can be the receiver of messages, be set and returned (as in the code example above).

By convention, Objective-C methods that have no other return value typically return **self**, so that nested message expressions are possible, as in:

```
    stuff = [[[List alloc] init] addObject:[[Bird alloc] init]];
```

In this example, **init** returns **self**, so that **addObject:** can be sent to the newly created instance in the same expression.

However, unnecessarily returning **self** can degrade the performance of Distributed Objects messages, so most OpenStep methods now return **void**.

Defining Classes

Before you begin implementing methods, you need to define a class. A class definition is separated into an interface file with the ".h" suffix and implementation file with the ".m" suffix. The interface file is the public declaration of instance variables and methods that other files may include, whereas the implementation file contains the actual code for each method.

Interface Files

Refer to the interface file below where MyClass inherits from MySuper-Class. A class interface file always imports its superclass interface file first. The directive **#import** is used instead of **#include** because it checks for multiple includes. Next the **@interface** directive is followed by the class name, a colon, and the superclass name. All instance variables must be declared between the following curly braces (as if the class were a C structure), and then followed by the method declarations and the **@end** directive.

```
#import "MySuperClass.h"

@interface MyClass:MySuperClass
{
    /* instance variables */
    id stuff;
    NSMutableString *title;
}
/* method declarations */
- init;
- (void)dealloc;
- stuff;
- addThing:anObject;
- (NSString *)title;
- (void)setTitle:(NSString *)str;

@end
```

Note that whenever the type is unspecified, it defaults to **id**. In the above example, the return value for the methods **stuff** and **addThing:** and the argument to **addThing:** all defaults to **id**.

Also, the compiler will not warn you if you omit the declaration of over-ridden methods, such as **init** which is inherited from NSObject. However, it is a good practice to list all methods the class implements as a form of documentation.

As stated earlier, all classes eventually inherit from the root class NSObject. Therefore, since MySuperClass is a direct subclass of NSObject, the interface file for MySuperClass looks like:

```
#import <Foundation/NSbject.h>

@interface MySuperClass:NSObject
{
    /* instance variables */
    ...
}
/* method declarations */
...

@end
```

It is an Objective-C convention to begin all class, category, and protocol names with an uppercase letter; and instance variables and methods with a lower case letter similar to Smalltalk. It is also a convention to name get and set methods after their corresponding instance variables, as in **title** and **setTitle:** (unlike C++, Objective-C does not confuse the **title** instance variable with the **title** method).

Implementation Files

Implementation files are structured similar to interface files. Refer to the implementation file for MyClass below. First, the interface file is imported along with any other header files, followed by the **@implementation** directive where the superclass and instance variable declarations are optional (omitted in this example), the method implementations and the **@end** directive.

The method implementations look like C functions within a pair of braces except for the leading "+" or "-," which indicates a class method versus an instance method.

```
#import "MyClass.h"
#import <Foundation/NSArray.h>

@implementation MyClass

- init
{
    [super init];
    stuff = [[NSMutableArray array] retain];
    return self;
}
```

```
- stuff
{
    return stuff;
}

- addThing:anObject
{
    [stuff addObjectIfAbsent:anObject];
    return self;
}

- (NSString *)title
{
    return title;
}

- (void)setTitle:(NSString *)str
{
    [title setString:str];
}

@end
```

Class Variables

Although class variables are not part of the Objective-C language, declaring a static variable in the implementation file and adding appropriate class methods can sometimes produce the desired effect. In this example, **count** behaves as a class variable and is used to keep track of the number of instances. The **instanceCount** class method simply returns **count**:

```
#import "AnotherClass.h"

static int count = 0;

@implementation AnotherClass

+ (int)instanceCount
{
    return count;
}
```

```
- init
{
    [super init];
    count++;
    return self;
}

@end
```

However, because **count** is really just a static variable, it can not be inherited by subclasses—it is only accessible via class methods defined by the parent class.

Shortcuts

Interface Builder can be used to quickly "draft" new classes, sometimes called "stubs." Within Interface Builder create a new subclass, add instance variables (called outlets), and methods (called actions). Interface Builder can then create the initial versions of the interface and implementation files for your new class.

Using Protocols

Protocols is a language feature unique to Objective-C that was originally added to support Distributed Objects. However, it turns out that protocols fix some deficiencies in Objective-C and promotes software reuse in ways that class inheritance can't. Protocols is a wonderful aid in designing modular systems that must incorporate third party components or interoperate with applications and services in a distributed environment.

A *protocol* is simply a list of methods, not attached to any specific class, that classes may conform to (provide implementations for the methods declared in the protocol).

Declaring a Protocol

Not surprising, a protocol declaration is similar to a class interface declaration, except there are no superclass and instance variables to declare as, in:

```
@protocol MyProtocol
- (BOOL)canYouFly;
- flyTo:destination;
@end
```

Adopting a Protocol

Classes can then adopt a protocol, or several protocols, by appending them to the interface declaration line (in the interface file) between angle brackets, as in:

```
@interface MyClass:MySuperClass < MyProtocol, YourProtocol >
...
@end
```

In this example, MyClass must provide an implementation for all the methods declared in MyProtocol and YourProtocol.

Querying Objects

You can then ask an anonymous object if it conforms to a particular protocol before sending it messages using the **conformsTo:** method inherited from NSObject, as in:

```
if ([anObject conformsTo:@protocol(MyProtocol)]) ...
```

Use With Distributed Objects

If you use Distributed Objects, you will want to establish formal protocols between your objects and remote objects. First of all, protocols define an interface without revealing implementation details of your classes, which is desirable when dealing with third parties (you only need to advertise the methods you want third parties to see). Secondly, protocols improves the efficiency of distributed messages by at least two-fold, since there is one less round-trip call needed if the message signatures of the remote objects are known.

Producing Mixins

Protocols have another advantage. By defining a protocol that multiple classes adopt, you produce an effect similar to mixins in the Common Lisp Object System (CLOS) (except that the method implementations are not shared). Using protocols in this way reduces the need for multiple inheritance in Objective-C, because unrelated classes can be typed alike simply because they share the same protocol.

Improving Type Checking

Protocols can also be used to improve compile time type checking which is normally limited in a dynamically typed language such as Objective-C. If you expect or require that an object conform to a particular protocol, you can annotate type declarations with the protocol, permitting the compiler to test for conformance, as in:

```
id <MyProtocol> anObject;
```

In this example, any messages sent to an object that are not part of MyProtocol will be caught by the compiler.

Protocol Examples

The best examples of protocol usage are in the Application Kit since it is a third party component that provides reusable mechanisms for objects not yet invented. For example, your objects can be dragged around with little programming effort by simply conforming to some protocols. (See protocol specs for NSDraggingInfo, NSDraggingDestination, and NSDraggingSource for details.)

Using Categories

Categories is another useful Objective-C language feature. Using categories, you can add method declarations and/or implementations to existing classes. Thus, you can extend existing classes without having the source code for those classes (for example, third party framework classes). Although you may rarely use this feature, categories are common in the OpenStep design, so you should at least understand how they work.

For example, some Application Kit classes add categories to Foundation Kit classes in support of Application Kit mechanisms. NSDraggingDestination and NSDraggingSource are really categories added to NSObject that add method declarations to NSObject. These kind of categories are referred to as *informal protocols*, because the interface they define is not enforced like real protocols.

You can also add method implementations to an existing class. For example, most delegate methods in the Application Kit are implemented as categories added to NSObject. These categories also add default implementation of the delegate methods so that delegates do not need to implement all delegate methods. Refer to specific Application Kit class specifications for details.

You declare a category as follows:

```
@interface NSObject (MyCategory)
- (BOOL)canYouFly;
- flyTo:destination;
@end
```

where MyCategory adds the **canYouFly** and **flyTo:** methods to NSObject. You implement category methods similarly:

```
@implementation NSObject (MyCategory)

- (BOOL)canYouFly
{
    ...
}

- flyTo:destination
{
    ...
}

@end
```

The convention is to add this declaration to an existing class interface file (for example, your class that uses these methods), or a new interface file named after the category (for example, **MyCategory.h**). Similarly, if there is an implementation of the category methods, they are added to an existing class implementation file or a new implementation file (for example, **MyCategory.m**).

You should be aware of some caveats when using categories. You normally use categories to add methods to an existing class, not override them—categories are not equivalent to subclasses. If you really need to override existing methods, keep in mind the following restrictions:

❑   You should not override methods declared in another category that was added to the same class. For example, if AnotherCategory was added to NSObject, then MyCategory should not override methods declared in AnotherCategory.

❑   You can incorporate the superclass's implementation (via a message to **super**), but you can't incorporate the class's implementation—you can't incorporate the method you are replacing.

If this is too restrictive, see NSObject's **poseAs:** class method. **poseAs:** allows you to override and add methods to an existing class with none of the above restrictions. Note, however, that neither categories nor **poseAs:** allows you to add instance variables to an existing class.

Programming With Nil

The keyword **nil** is defined as a null object. In C language terms, it is an **id** with a value of 0. Instance variables typed **id** that have not been assigned a value are initialized to **nil**. It is also possible for methods to return a **nil** object, especially if the method deallocates the receiver.

Normally a runtime error occurs (unless caught) if an object receives a message that it does not have an implementation for. But messages sent to **nil** do nothing—they simply return **nil**. This behavior and usage of **nil** results in a unique style of programming—you don't need to check the return value of some methods, as in:

```
anObject = [aDictionary objectForKey:aKey];
[anObject flyHome];
```

If **objectForKey:** returns **nil** because there is no object with that key, then sending **flyHome** to **anObject** will not cause the program to crash. Sometimes a **nil** return value is perfectly reasonable—it should not be treated as an exception.

Booch Lite

C

The Booch Notation incorporates aspects of both the Jacobson (OOSE) and Rumbaugh (OMT) methods, and the notation is now in the public domain to support a standard representation of OO designs. The notation is very complete, provides various levels of detail, and is well suited for hybrid OO languages such as Objective-C. Because of this versatility, the Booch Notation can be used in combination with most any OO design method.

The Booch Notation stresses the importance of representing both static and dynamic aspects of the design. The notation separates the design into logical and physical views, and static and dynamic semantics. Logical views describe the key abstractions that form the OO design. Class and object diagrams are examples of logical views. Physical views describe the concrete software and hardware components of the implementation. Module and process diagrams are examples of physical views.

Static views show the relationship of components and dynamic views describe the actual runtime behavior. Class and object diagrams show the relationship between objects such as class inheritance and part-whole. State transition diagrams specifically focus on runtime behavior. Also, object and interaction diagrams can show the dynamic flow of messages between objects.

This book uses *Booch Lite*, just the essentials, with the exception of a few advanced features. We also interpret the notation for Objective-C programming. For example, the role adornment in class and object diagrams is used to denote a class or object that conforms to an Objective-C protocol.

This appendix covers class, class categories, object, interaction, module, and process diagrams (state transition diagrams are not used in this book). For a complete description of the Booch Notation and Booch Lite see *Object-Oriented Analysis and Design With Applications* by Grady Booch.

Class Diagrams

The *class diagram* is a logical static view that shows the relationships between classes, including inheritance and part-whole relationships.

Class Icon

A class is denoted by a cloud or what I like to call an amoeba (a microscopic animal that multiplies similar to a factory object in Objective-C and Smalltalk) shown in Figure C–1. The boundary of the class icon is dashed to suggest an abstraction, as opposed to an instance which has a solid boundary.

Figure C–1   Class icon.

The name of the class is placed in the center of the amoeba, and any interesting attributes or operations may be listed. An attribute's name, class, or both may be specified using the syntax in Table C–1. The class may also be adorned with an "A" within a triangle to indicate an abstract class, one without instances.

Table C–1   Attribute Syntax

SYNTAX	DESCRIPTION
A	Name only.
: C	Class only.
A : C	Name and class.
A : C = E	Name, class and default expression.

Relationships

Lines are then used to connect classes and depict specific types of relationships such as inheritance or "is a," "has," "using," and other generic associations (see Table C–2). When depicting inheritance, the arrow head points from the subclass to the superclass, as in Figure C–2, where View inherits from Responder. However, when denoting the "has" and "using" relationships, the circle ending is on the side that "has," as a part, or uses the other class. Any relationship (other than inheritance) can be further annotated with cardinality placed on the target side of the association. For example, in Figure C–2, View has one **superview**, one list of **subviews**, and one **window**, but NSArray has zero or more objects.

Table C–2   Class Relationships

GRAPHIC	DESCRIPTION
	Association
➤	Inheritance
•———	Has
○———	Using

Note, the "has" relationship typically implies that the class on the *whole* end of the relationship will have an instance variable containing an instance of the class on the *part* end. The line can even be labeled with the name of the instance variable if it is known. In contrast, the "using" relationship is sort of a "catch all" as Booch describes:

> *The "using" icon denotes a client/supplier relationship, . . . It is typically used to indicate the decision that operations of the client class invoke operations of the supplier class, or have signatures whose return class or arguments are instances of the supplier class.*

If the relationship is unspecified, then the classes are simply connected by a line with no adornments on either end.

Figure C–2   Example class diagram.

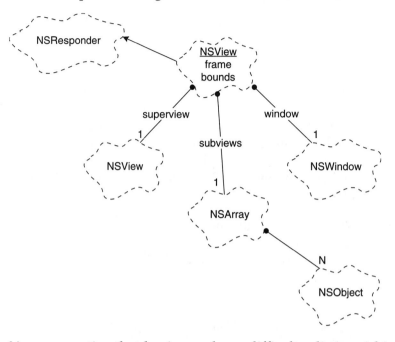

You may notice that beginners have difficulty distinguishing between the concepts of class inheritance and part-whole relationships; it is confusing to see both of these relationships on the same diagram. Also, it is natural to identify part-whole relationships first, and class inheritance last. We recommend not mixing class inheritance and part-whole in the same diagram, and in most cases, a simple text and line diagram will suffice to show class inheritance, as in Figure C–3.

Figure C–3   Example class hierarchy.

Containment

The physical containment adornment differentiates containment by value and containment by reference. In some languages, instance variables can be statically typed (contained by value) as **foo** is in this Objective-C example:

```
MyClass    foo;    /* by value */
id    anObject;    /* by reference */
```

The physical containment adornment is a box on the target side of a relationship. A filled box indicates containment by value and an open box indicates containment by reference.

Containment is really an implementation detail—most statically typed instance variables are private anyway. Also, in Objective-C containment by reference is most common. Therefore, the containment adornment is not used in this book. You may assume that all associations illustrated in this book are by reference.

Class Utilities

Because Objective-C and C++ are hybrid languages, you may need an icon to represent a group of functions which Booch calls *class utilities*. The class utility icon is similar to a class icon but has a grey shadow, as in Figure C–4. A class utility may also be a class that only has class variables and methods, not any instances, in which case it acts as a global instance. By definition, classes may associate with and use class utilities, but not inherit from or contain an instance of a class utility.

Figure C–4   Class utilities icon.

Although it is possible to implement a class utility as a global instance in both Objective-C and C++, it is not desirable because it is not extensible. Sometimes it is better to design a class so that it can be instantiated, even though it may only have one instance (for example, NSApp is a global instance of NSApplication, not a class). Often, you can not anticipate the future requirements of your system. If later you find you need two or more instances of the class, you will have to redesign the class.

Roles

Booch also provides a way to denote the roles an object plays:

> *...the role of an abstraction is the face it presents to the world at a given moment. A role denotes the purpose or capacity wherein one class associates with another.*

For Objective-C, you can interpret a role to be the same as a formal or informal protocol that defines interfaces between objects. Therefore, Objective-C protocols will be denoted on class diagrams by placing a textual adornment to the side of the relationship that conforms to that protocol. Figure C–5 illustrates the dragging mechanism where NSDraggingSource and NSDraggingDestination are informal protocols and NSDraggingInfo is a formal protocol.

Figure C–5   Dragging mechanism class diagram.

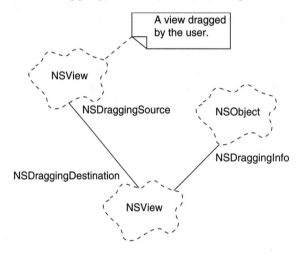

Notes

Finally, textual notes that provide more information can be attached to class diagrams or specifically to any item using a dashed line, as in Figure C–5.

Class Categories

Class categories are logical groupings of classes that may or may not coincide with a software module. (Class categories are not the same as Objective-C categories.) Class categories are themselves tightly coupled but only loosely coupled to one another. As Booch points out, some of the classes are public, thus defining the external interface and others are private, part of the implementation.

Class categories are depicted by a box containing the name and, optionally, a listing of the interesting classes contained within (see Figure C–6). Because class categories are a higher level of abstraction than a class, the same "using" adornment, the open circle, is used to denote the dependencies between class categories. A dependency indicates that classes on the "using" side of the relationship may inherit from, contain instances of, use, or associate with classes on the other side. Class categories that are used throughout the design (for example, common classes like NSObject in Objective-C) are labeled with the word "global" and placed at the bottom to simplify diagrams.

Figure C–6   Example class categories.

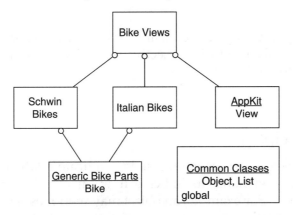

Object Diagrams

Object diagrams are used to capture the relationships between instances at a particular moment in time and the message flow between objects. They are not intended to document the complete state of a program, but focus on only the interesting aspects of the design—the mechanisms that exhibit patterns of behavior.

Object Icon

An object icon is similar to a class icon but has a solid boundary and contains the name of the object and any interesting attributes previously shown in Figure C–7. The name of the object uses similar syntax for class attributes shown in Table C–1. For example, you might use ":NSArray" instead of "aCollection" to specifically indicate that the object was an instance of NSArray, but is otherwise anonymous. You would give an object icon a unique name if it represents a specific instance, such as a global (for example NSApp).

Figure C–7   Object icon.

Object diagrams may also contain class utilities, metaclasses, and class icons (especially useful in Objective-C implementations where classes are also factory objects).

Relationships

Lines between object icons are used to indicate relationships. Lines are adorned with symbols to indicate how an object is made visible to another object. For example, an object may send messages to objects that it uses in its implementation or are part of the whole (an object instance variable). The visibility is indicated by a box containing a letter on the side of the receiving object. The letters which are used to indicate different types of visibilities appear in Table C–1.

Table C–3   Visibility Adornments

SYMBOL	DESCRIPTION
G	The receiver is global to the sender.
P	The receiver is a parameter to some operation of the sender.
F	The receiver is a field of the sender (e.g., an instance variable).
L	The receiver is locally declared within the scope of the object diagram

An example of object relationships and the visibility adornment is illustrated in Figure C–8.

Message Flow

Object diagrams can also be annotated to show the message flow between objects. This feature is what distinguishes object diagrams from class diagrams.

Lines that connect objects are labeled with the message, direction of invocation and optionally a sequence number. The return value, name and actual arguments may be given for each message if necessary (preferably using the syntax of the implementation language). For example, Figure C–8 shows the message flow resulting from sending **display:** to an instance of NSView that has two subviews. This diagram captures an important aspect about displaying views. Superviews are drawn before subviews, and it is the **drawRect:** method that should be overridden to customize a view, not the **display:** method.

Figure C–8   Message flow example.

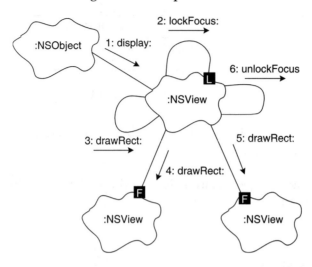

Roles

Similar to class diagrams, relationships can be adorned with a role (or protocol in Objective-C). The name of the role appears on the side of the relationship that conforms to that role.

Concurrency and Synchronization

When using Distributed Objects, concurrency and synchronization are important aspects that also need to be captured in an object diagram.

An object icon may be adorned with one of the names in Table C–4 to specify the concurrency semantics. Most often you will simply use "active" to denote root objects that are available to receive distributed messages. The object is assumed to be sequential, if the concurrency is unspecified.

Table C–4   Concurrency Types

TYPE	DESCRIPTION
active	Object embodies own thread of control.
guarded	Object semantics are guaranteed in the presence of multiple active objects but active objects must collaborate to achieve mutual exclusion.
sequential	Object semantics are guaranteed only in the presence of a single active object at one time.
synchronous	Object semantics are guaranteed in the presence of multiple active objects, but the active objects must guarantee mutual exclusion.

To specify the synchronization, the simple arrow that indicates the direction of invocation is replaced with one of the symbols in Table C-5.

Table C–5   Synchronization Icons

SYMBOL	DESCRIPTION
× ➤	Synchronous
➘	Asynchronous (oneway)
🕐 ➤	Timeout
◄	Balking, return immediately if not serviced

Interaction Diagrams

An interaction diagram also models the message flow between objects, and is an alternative to using object diagrams. The advantage of using an interaction diagram is that it can be annotated with the text from a script to improve understanding and provide some traceability in the method you use. Also, interaction diagrams can be used to show the focus of control explained below. However, interaction diagrams are not equivalent to object diagrams. Object diagrams may contain more information about links between objects, attribute values, roles, etc. Because a simple interaction diagram provides no more information than an object diagram, only the advanced features will be presented here.

An interaction diagram has a tabular form with objects listed horizontally across the top and time increasing vertically as in Figure C–9. A vertical dotted line is drawn under each object, and messages are drawn horizontally from dotted line to dotted line indicating communication between the corresponding objects where the message syntax is similar to object diagrams. Time increases in the vertical direction with the first message shown at the top and the last at the bottom of the diagram.

In addition, interaction diagrams can be annotated with descriptive text of each action in the left margin. You may number the actions, but they do not have to correspond to individual messages. Also, the focus of control is indicated by drawing a block on the object's dotted line for the period that object is in control. Messages drawn from a block are under the control of that object, or within the scope of the message that initiated the block. For example, in Figure C–9, all of the messages sent after the initial **display:** are within the scope of NSView's **display:** method. Object diagrams, on the other hand, do not show focus of control explicitly—focus of control is implied.

Figure C–9   Example interaction diagram.

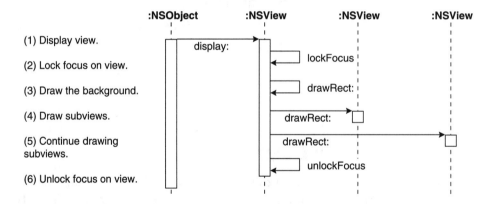

Although not standard, the concurrency and synchronization adornments can also be used with interaction diagrams. When showing multiple processes or threads of control, you can enclose objects that belong in the same process using a rectangle, as shown in Figure C–10. In this diagram, **agentDidChangeTitle:** and **indexDidChangeAgents:** are asynchronous messages.

Figure C–10 Example interaction diagram showing synchronization.

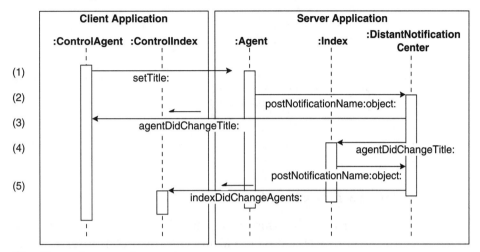

(1)   Change the name of an agent.

(2)   The agent notifies dependents.

(3)   The agent's control object is notified.

(4)   The index is notified.

(5)   The index's control object is notified.

Module Diagrams

In Booch terminology, a *module* is a physical unit corresponding to a source file. A module may be the main program file, the header file (specification) or implementation file (body). Modules are then grouped together into more manageable units called *subsystems* that correspond to software libraries. Although Booch provides a notation for modules, it is too fine grained for our purposes, so only the top level module diagram depicting the relationship between subsystems is presented here.

A subsystem is denoted by a rounded rectangle with a shadow containing its name, as in Figure C–11. Dependencies between subsystems are shown by a directed arrow. In practice, subsystem dependencies must be directed trees, otherwise it will be nearly impossible to compile the code!

Figure C–11 Example module diagram.

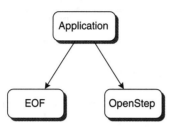

Process Diagrams

A process diagram shows the physical separation of processors, devices, and processes; where a processor is a computer, a device is other hardware not capable of running programs, and a process is a computer program (for example, an application or service). Process diagrams contain processor and device icons connected together to represent communication links, as shown in Figure C–12, where the shadowed icon is a processor and the other a device. Both icons contain the name of the entity, but a processor can be adorned with a list of the processes that it will run. Communication links can be labeled and if a link is one way, an arrow may be added to show the direction of the link.

Figure C–12 Example process diagram.

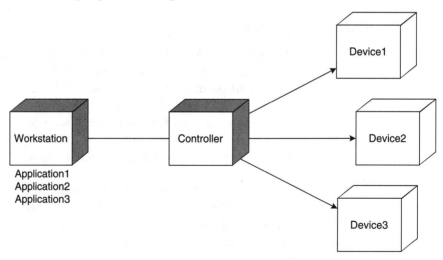

Process diagrams do not explicitly show the interaction between processes as one might expect. However, when using Distributed Objects in Objective-C, processes communicate by first establishing connections to root objects that have been published to the Network Name Server. Therefore, object diagrams featuring these root objects and using the concurrency and synchronization adornments described above, accompanied by a process diagram, are sufficient to provide a complete picture of the interprocess communication. See Chapter 7—*Distributed Objects* for more examples.

Class Specifications   D

This appendix documents important entity and control objects used in the implementation of the groupware version of the Cards application. Since not all aspects of the groupware implementation were covered in Chapter 6—*Implementation* and Chapter 7—*Distributed Objects*, these class specifications differ slightly from the class interfaces previously presented in this book.

These class specifications also correspond to the source files on the enclosed CD and should be used as reference when examining or modifying the code. Source code comments do not repeat material covered in this appendix—they only clarify implementation details not covered here.

The major software components are:

❑   The *Model Framework* containing all entity object and other classes shared by the Cards and CardsServer applications.

❑   The *Cards* application, the client side or frontend, consisting of all control and interface objects.

❑   The *CardsServer* application, the server side or backend, consisting of all entity objects including the root Session object.

Since the CardsServer application is fairly trivial, only the Model Framework and Cards application classes are documented in this appendix.

Model Framework Classes

The Model Framework contains entity object classes that model persistent information shown in Figure D-1. This framework is used by both the Cards client application and the CardsServer application. If a groupware session is active, instances of these objects are remote, located in

191

the CardsServer application. Otherwise, they are local to the client when operating in single user model.

Figure D–1   Model framework class hierarchy.

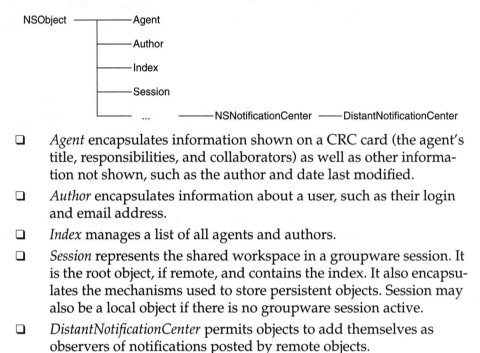

❑   *Agent* encapsulates information shown on a CRC card (the agent's title, responsibilities, and collaborators) as well as other information not shown, such as the author and date last modified.

❑   *Author* encapsulates information about a user, such as their login and email address.

❑   *Index* manages a list of all agents and authors.

❑   *Session* represents the shared workspace in a groupware session. It is the root object, if remote, and contains the index. It also encapsulates the mechanisms used to store persistent objects. Session may also be a local object if there is no groupware session active.

❑   *DistantNotificationCenter* permits objects to add themselves as observers of notifications posted by remote objects.

Cards Application Classes

The Cards application classes include control object classes that act as intermediaries between entity objects and interface objects (instances of NSView and NSWindow created using Interface Builder). Control object classes are shown in Figure D-2.

Figure D–2   Cards application class hierarchy.

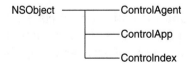

❑ *ControlAgent* is the control object class for Agent objects. It is the target of buttons and controls located on the CRC card window. It updates its model whenever the user makes changes, and conversely updates the display whenever the model changes (possibly initiated by another user's action).

❑ *ControlApp* is the control object for the entire application. There's only one ControlApp object per Cards application. It's the delegate of NSApp and the target of menu items. It manages connections to the Session object if it is remote, otherwise creates and deletes the local Session object. It also creates the ControlIndex corresponding to the Index entity object managed by the Session object.

❑ *ControlIndex* is the control object class for Index objects. It is the target of buttons and controls located on the index window. It modifies its model when the user makes changes (for example, if the user deletes an agent), and conversely updates its display if the model or any of the agents change (for example, updates the modification date if a user changes an agent's responsibilities text).

Note, ControlIndex and ControlAgent objects own themselves. They release themselves and close their windows when their models are deleted. They observe model notifications and are notified when their models are about to be deleted.

However, ControlIndex objects behave slightly differently when their models are about to be deleted. Since the ControlIndex window represents the document, ControlIndex sends **close:** to the ControlApp object, allowing the user to save changes before closing (The ControlApp object is NSApp's delegate). ControlIndex objects are then released only when their models are deleted. See the ControlIndex class specification for details.

Agent

Inherits From: NSObject

Conforms To: NSObject (NSObject)
                    NSCoding

Class Description

Agent objects manage information displayed on a CRC card: the agent's title, description of its responsibilities, and a list of its collaborating agents. It also maintains other information, such as the author of the card and the date it was last modified. Instances of Agent, hereafter called *agents*, are entity objects that model persistent information. See the ControlAgent class specification for a description of an agent's corresponding control and interface objects.

Agents post notifications when any of its data changes or when it's about to be deleted (see *Notifications* below). Control objects and other entity objects, such as Index objects, observe these notifications. For example, agents observe ObjectWillDeleteNotifications posted by their collaborating agents and will remove them from their list of collaborators. Agents post an AgentDidChangeCollaboratorsNotification whenever their list of collaborators changes. ControlAgent objects observe this notification and update their displays accordingly.

Adopted Protocols

NSCoding
     – encodeWithCoder:
     – initWithCoder:

Method Types

Set and get methods
     – title
     – setTitle:
     – responsibilities
     – setResponsibilities:
     – collaborators
     – addCollaborators:
     – removeCollaborators:
     – author
     – setAuthor:
     – date
     – setDate:
     – defaultCenter

Notification messages	– agentDidChangeTitle: – willDelete:
Deleting an Agent	– delete
Locking an Agent	– lock: – unlock: – isLocked

Instance Methods

addCollaborators:

– (void)**addCollaborators:**(NSArray *)*anArray*

Adds the agents contained in *anArray* to the receiver's collaborators, sorts them alphabetically, and changes the modification date. Posts an AgentDidChangeCollaboratorsNotification so that control objects can update their displays.

See also: **– collaborators, – removeCollaborators:**

agentDidChangeTitle:

– (void)**agentDidChangeTitle:**(NSNotification *)*notification*

Invoked when a collaborator's title has changed. Sorts the receiver's collaborators alphabetically and posts an AgentDidChangeCollaborators-Notification so that control objects can update their displays.

author

– (id)**author**

Returns the receiver's author.

See also: **– setAuthor:**

collaborators

– (NSArray *)**collaborators**

Returns the receiver's collaborators (containing Agent objects).

See also: – **addCollaborators:**, – **removeCollaborators:**

date

  – (NSDate *)**date**

Returns the date the receiver was last modified.

See also: – **setDate:**

defaultCenter

  – (NSNotificationCenter *)**defaultCenter**

Returns the notification center that the receiver will use to post notifications. Use this method to observe notifications from the receiver.

See also: + **defaultCenter** (DistantNotificationCenter)

delete

  – (void)**delete**

Posts an ObjectWillDeleteNotification so that control objects can take the appropriate action (for example, remove interface objects from the display and release themselves).

isLocked

  – (BOOL)**isLocked**

Returns YES if the receiver is locked, NO otherwise.

lock:

  – (BOOL)**lock:**(id)*anAuthor*

Locks the receiver for editing by *anAuthor*. If successful sets the receiver's author to *anAuthor*, posts an AgentDidChangeLockNotification and returns YES, otherwise, returns NO.

removeCollaborators:

   – (void)**removeCollaborators:**(NSArray *)*anArray*

Removes the agents in *anArray* from the receiver's collaborators, and changes the modification date. Posts an AgentDidChangeCollaborators-Notification so that control objects can update their displays.

See also: **– addCollaborators:, – collaborators**

responsibilities

   – (NSString *)**responsibilities**

Returns a description of the receiver's responsibilities.

See also: **– setResponsibilities:**

setAuthor:

   – (void)**setAuthor:**(id)*anAuthor*

Sets the receiver's author to *anAuthor*, and changes the modification date. Posts an AgentDidChangeAuthorNotification so that control objects can update their displays.

See also: **– author**

setDate:

   – (void)**setDate:**(NSDate *)*newDate*

Sets the receiver's modification date to *newDate*. Posts an AgentDid-ChangeDateNotification so that control objects can update their displays.

See also: **– date**

setResponsibilities:

   – (void)**setResponsibilities:**(NSString *)*aString*

Sets the description of the receiver's responsibilities to *aString*, and changes the modification date. Posts an AgentDidChangeResponsibili-tiesNotification so that control objects can update their displays.

See also: – responsibilities

setTitle:

– (void)**setTitle:**(NSString *)*aString*

Sets the receiver's title to *aString,* and changes the modification date. Posts an AgentDidChangeTitleNotification so that control objects can update their displays.

See also: – title

title

– (NSString *)**title**

Returns the receiver's title.

See also: – setTitle:

unlock:

– (BOOL)**unlock:**(id)*anAuthor*

Unlocks the receiver if it was locked by *anAuthor.* If successful posts an AgentDidChangeLockNotification and returns YES, otherwise returns NO.

willDelete:

– (void)**willDelete:**(NSNotification *)*notification*

Invoked when a collaborator is about to be deleted. Removes the notifying object, an Agent object, from the receiver's collaborators.

Notifications

AgentDidChangeAuthorNotification

Notification Object   An Agent

Posted when an agent's author changes.

AgentDidChangeCollaboratorsNotification

Notification Object   An Agent

Posted when an agent's collaborators changes. For example, collaborators are added or removed, or the order changes.

AgentDidChangeDateNotification

Notification Object   An Agent

Posted when an agent's modification date changes.

AgentDidChangeLockNotification

Notification Object   An Agent

Posted when an agent's lock state changes.

AgentDidChangeResponsibilitiesNotification

Notification Object   An Agent

Posted when an agent's responsibilities text changes.

AgentDidChangeTitleNotification

Notification Object   An Agent

Posted when an agent's title changes.

ObjectWillDeleteNotification

Notification Object   An Agent

Posted when an agent is about to be deleted.

Author

Inherits From: NSObject

Conforms To: NSObject (NSObject)
                   NSCoding

Class Description

The Author class simply encapsulates information about a user such as their login name and email address. Most of the information about an author is currently not used by the Cards application. Ideally, information about authors (perhaps an author database) is a service available to all applications. This class could also be enhanced to store more information about authors useful for groupware sessions, such as permissions and workgroups.

Adopted Protocols

NSCoding   – encodeWithCoder:
                                  – initWithCoder:

Method Types

Set and get methods   – emailAddress
                                  – setEmailAddress:
                                  – firstName
                                  – setFirstName:
                                  – lastName:
                                  – setLastName:
                                  – loginName
                                  – setLoginName:
                                  – officeLocation
                                  – setOfficeLocation:
                                  – phone
                                  – setPhone:
                                  – defaultCenter

Instance Methods

defaultCenter

– (NSNotificationCenter *)**defaultCenter**

Returns the notification center that the receiver will use to post notifications. Use this method to observe notifications from the receiver.

See also: + **defaultCenter** (DistantNotificationCenter)

emailAddress

– (NSString *)**emailAddress**

Returns the receiver's email address.

See also: – **setEmailAddress:**

firstName

– (NSString *)**firstName**

Returns the receiver's first name.

See also: – **setFirstName:**

lastName

– (NSString *)**lastName**

Returns the receiver's last name.

See also: – **setLastName:**

loginName

– (NSString *)**loginName**

Returns the receiver's login name.

See also: – **setLoginName:**

officeLocation

> – (NSString *)**officeLocation**

Returns the receiver's office location.

See also: – **setOfficeLocation:**

phone

> – (NSString *)**phone**

Returns the receiver's phone number.

See also: – **setPhone:**

setEmailAddress:

> – (void)**setEmailAddress:**(NSString *)*aString*

Sets the receiver's email address to *aString*.

See also: – **emailAddress**

setFirstName:

> – (void)**setFirstName:**(NSString *)*aString*

Sets the receiver's first name to *aString*.

See also: – **firstName**

setLastName:

> – (void)**setLastName:**(NSString *)*aString*

Sets the receiver's last name to *aString*.

See also: – **lastName**

setLoginName:

> – (void)**setLoginName:**(NSString *)*aString*

Sets the receiver's login name to *aString*.

See also: – **loginName**

setOfficeLocation:

    – (void)**setOfficeLocation:**(NSString *)*aString*

Sets the receiver's office location to *aString*.

See also: – **officeLocation**

setPhone:

    – (void)**setPhone:**(NSString *)*aString*

Sets the receiver's phone number to *aString*.

See also: – **phone**

ControlAgent

Inherits From: NSObject

Conforms To: NSObject (NSObject)
                      NSDraggingDestination
                      NSNibAwaking
                      NSTableDataSource

Class Description

A ControlAgent is the control object for an Agent object. It acts as the intermediary between its model, an instance of Agent, and its interface objects (NSView and NSWindow objects created using Interface Builder).

A ControlAgent handles user actions such as adding and removing collaborators and editing the title and responsibilities text fields. A ControlAgent is the target and receiver of action messages setup using Interface Builder—it is the owner of **ControlAgent.nib**. These action methods update the state of the model to reflect changes made by the user.

Conversely, ControlAgents observe change notifications posted by their models and update their displays accordingly. For example, if another user changes the title of a ControlAgent's model then it is notified and updates the display.

ControlAgents are also the delegates of their NSWindow objects and are notified before their windows are closed. ControlAgents own themselves and therefore release themselves if their window is closed or their model is deleted (see **willDelete:** and **windowWillClose:**).

Adopted Protocols

NSDraggingDestination	– concludeDragOperation: – draggingEntered: – draggingExited: – performDragOperation:
NSNibAwaking	– awakeFromNib

NSTableDataSource	– numberOfRowsInTableView:
	– tableView:
	   objectValueForTableColumn:
	   row:

Method Types

Set and get methods	– model – setModel: – selectedAgents – window
Action messages	– ok: – open: – removeCollaborators: – revert: – lockAction:
Agent notifications	– agentDidChangeCollaborators: – agentDidChangeTitle: – agentDidChangeResponsibilities: – agentDidChangeLock: – willDelete:

NSTableView notifications   – selectionChanged:

NSText delegate messages   – textDidEndEditing:

NSWindow delegate messages   – windowWillClose:

Instance Methods

agentDidChangeCollaborators:

– (void)**agentDidChangeCollaborators:**(NSNotification *)*notification*

Invoked when the receiver's model changes its collaborators. Updates the receiver's interface objects.

agentDidChangeLock:

– (void)**agentDidChangeLock:**(NSNotification*)*notification*

Invoked when the receiver's model changes its lock state. Updates the receiver's interface.

agentDidChangeResponsibilities:

– (void)**agentDidChangeResponsibilities:**(NSNotification *)*notification*

Invoked when the receiver's model changes its responsibilities text. Updates the receiver's interface objects.

agentDidChangeTitle:

– (void)**agentDidChangeTitle:**(NSNotification *)*notification*

Invoked when the receiver's model changes its title. Updates the receiver's interface objects.

lockAction:

– (void)**lockAction:**(id)*sender*

Attempts to lock or unlock the receiver's model.

model

    – (id)**model**

Returns the receiver's model.

See also: – **setModel:**

ok:

    – (void)**ok:**(id)*sender*

Sets the model's title to the text entered by the user.

open:

    – (void)**open:**(id)*sender*

Opens the window corresponding to the selected collaborator.

See also: – **openAgent:** (ControlApp), – **selectedAgent**

removeCollaborators:

    – (void)**removeCollaborators:**(id)*sender*

Removes the collaborators selected by the user from the model.

revert:

    – (void)**revert:**(id)*sender*

Reverts the interface objects to the state of the receiver's model.

selectedAgents

    – (NSArray *)**selectedAgents**

Returns the agents (instances of Agent) that the user selected from the collaborator table.

See also: – **open:**

selectionChanged:

   – (void)**selectionChanged:**(NSNotification *)*notification*

Invoked when the collaborator table selection changes, and updates the receiver's folder icon accordingly.

setModel:

   – (void)**setModel:**(id)*anObject*

Sets the receiver's model to *anObject*. The receiver releases the old model if it exists and retains the new model (necessary when the model is remote). Adds itself as an observer of change notifications posted by the new model.

See also: – **model**

textDidEndEditing:

   – (void)**textDidEndEditing:**(NSNotification *)*notification*

Invoked when the user finished editing the responsibilities NSText object. Sets the model's responsibilities to the new text entered by the user.

willDelete:

   – (void)**willDelete:**(NSNotification *)*notification*

Closes the receiver's window be sending it the **performClose:** message. **performClose:** will notify the window's delegate (the receiver).

See also: – **windowWillClose:**

window

   – (id)**window**

Returns the receiver's NSWindow object.

windowWillClose:

    – (void)**windowWillClose:**(NSNotification *)*notification*

Invoked when the receiver's window is about to be closed. Releases the receiver (the receiver owns itself). The window will release itself on closure.

See also: – willDelete:

ControlApp

Inherits From: NSObject

Conforms To: NSObject (NSObject)
               NSMenuValidation

Class Description

A ControlApp object is a high-level control object for the entire Cards application. Since there is only one ControlApp object per application process, it is simply called *the ControlApp*. Note, the CardsServer application uses a different ControlApp class—this class specification only documents the client's ControlApp class used by the Cards application.

The ControlApp is NSApp's delegate and handles setup when the application is first launched and cleanup when the application is terminated. ControlApp implements the NSApplication delegate method **application:openFile:**, allowing the user to double-click on a Cards document to launch the application (any document ending with ".cards"). ControlApp implements **applicationWillTerminate:** to prompt the user before terminating the application allowing the user to save any changes.

The ControlApp is also the target of action messages sent by the main menu (set using Interface Builder). ControlApp implements a single document style user interface allowing the user to create, open and close documents. The ControlApp owns a single Session object that encapsulates the mechanism used to store persistent objects.

ControlApp also provides action methods for creating, opening and closing groupware sessions. When the application is first launched, a local Session object is created. The remote operations work as follows:

❑   If the user creates a new groupware session, the local Session object is released, the CardsServer application is launched, and a connection is made to the remote Session object.

❑   If the user opens a groupware session (wishes to join in on an existing session), then the local Session object is released, and a connection is made to the existing CardsServer if it is running.

❑   When a remote session is closed, it is released and a local Session object is created (used to emulate single user mode).

Currently, you can only open one session at a time, and must close an existing session before creating or opening a new session.

Note, the user needs to know the "password," the name of the root object, to connect to an existing remote Session object. A group of users can agree on a password and therefore exclude others from joining their groupware session. Users can change the password at any time, see the Session class specification for details.

Adopted Protocols

NSMenuValidation	– validateMenuItem:

Method Types

Set and get methods	– setSession:
	– newControlIndex
	– cascadeWindow:
	– index
Opening an agent	– openAgent:
Info menu actions	– openInfoPanel:
File menu actions	– open:
	– new:
	– save:
	– saveAs:
	– revertToSaved:
	– close:

Cards menu actions	– newAgent:
Session menu actions	– openSession: – newSession: – closeSession:
Session notifications	– indexDidChange:
NSApplication delegate messages	– application:openFile: – applicationOpenUntitledFile: – applicationWillTerminate:
NSConnection notifications	– connectionDidDie:

Instance Methods

application:openFile:

> – (BOOL)**application:**(NSApplication *)*theApp*
> **openFile:**(NSString *)*filename*

Sends **openFile:** to the receiver's Session object passing *filename* as the argument.

applicationOpenUntitledFile:

> – (BOOL)**applicationOpenUntitledFile:**(NSApplication *)*theApp*

Simply sends **new:** to the receiver to open a new file.

applicationWillTerminate:

> – (void)**applicationWillTerminate:**(NSNotification *)*notification*

If the Session object is local, sends **close:** to the receiver allowing the user to save changes to the document before quitting. If the Session object is remote, sets it to **nil** and posts a SessionWillCloseNotification. Local control objects should observe this notification and delete themselves.

cascadeWindow:

> – (void)**cascadeWindow:**(NSWindow *)*window*

Positions *window* cascaded to the lower right of the last window positioned by this method.

close:

– (void)**close:**(id)*sender*

If the document was edited, allows the user to save changes before closing the document. Sends **closeFile:** to the receiver's Session object.

See also: – **new:**, – **open:**, – **revertToSaved:**, – **save:**, – **saveAs:**

closeSession:

– (void)**closeSession:**(id)*sender*

Closes the current groupware session and returns to single user mode, where the Session object is local, not remote. Posts a SessionWillClose-Notificaton so that local control objects can delete themselves.

See also: – **newSession:**, – **openSession:**

index

– (id)**index**

Returns the Session object's index.

See also: –**newControlIndex:**

indexDidChange:

– (void)**indexDidChange:**(NSNotification *)*notification*

Invoked when the receiver's Session changes its Index object. Creates a new ControlIndex corresponding to the new Index object.

See also: – **newControlIndex:**

new:

– (void)**new:**(id)*sender*

Closes the current document by invoking **close:** and creates a new index by sending **newIndex** to the receiver's Session object.

See also: – **close:**, – **open:**, – **revertToSaved:**, – **save:**, – **saveAs:**

newAgent:

> – (void)**newAgent:**(id)*sender*

Creates a new Agent object, adds it to the Session's Index object, creates a corresponding ControlAgent object, and opens its window.

newControlIndex

> – (void)**newControlIndex**

Creates a new ControlIndex object with the Session's Index object as the model. Positions and displays the ControlIndex's window.

newSession:

> – (void)**newSession:**(id)*sender*

Opens a new groupware session by launching the CardsServer application, makes a connection to its remote Session object, and sets the root object's name to the password specified by the user. If successful, the old Session object is released, its index is closed, and a new "empty" index appears corresponding to the remote Session object.

See also: – **closeSession:**, – **openSession:**

open:

> – (void)**open:**(id)*sender*

Opens a new document selected by the user by sending **openFile:** to the receiver's Session object. If successful, the Session object will post a SessionDidChangeIndexNotification, invoking the receiver's **indexDidChange:** method. Consequently, the old Index is closed and the new Index is opened.

See also: – **new:**, – **close:**, – **revertToSaved:**, – **save:**, – **saveAs:**

openAgent:

> – (void)**openAgent:**(id)*agent*

Opens the window corresponding to *agent*. If no window can be found, creates a new ControlAgent for *agent* and opens its window.

openInfoPanel:

    – (void)**openInfoPanel:**(id)*sender*

Opens the receiver's information panel.

openSession:

    – (void)**openSession:**(id)*sender*

Opens a connection to an existing groupware session using the password specified by the user. If successful, the old Session object is released, its index is closed, and a new index appears corresponding to the remote Session object.

See also: – **closeSession:**, – **newSession:**

revertToSaved:

    – (void)**revertToSaved:**(id)*sender*

Reverts the document to the last version saved by sending **openFile:** to the receiver's Session object. If successful, the Session object will post a SessionDidChangeIndexNotification, invoking the receiver's **indexDid-Change:** method. Consequently, the old index is closed and the new index is opened.

See also: – **new:**, – **close:**, – **open:**, – **save:**, – **saveAs:**

save:

    – (void)**save:**(id)*sender*

Saves the document using the current filename by sending **saveFile:** to the receiver's Session object.

See also: – **new:**, – **close:**, – **open:**, – **revertToSaved:**, – **saveAs:**

saveAs:

    – (void)**saveAs:**(id)*sender*

Uses the shared SavePanel to save the document using a new filename specified by the user. Sends **saveFile:** to the receiver's Session object.

See also: – **new:**, – **close:**, – **open:**, – **revertToSaved:**, – **save:**

setSession:

– (void)**setSession:**(id)*aSession*

Sets the receiver's session object to *aSession* by releasing the old Session object and retaining the new one. Creates a new ControlIndex object by invoking **newControlIndex**, registers for Session object notifications, and application deaths if *aSession* is remote.

Notifications

SessionWillCloseNitification

Notification Object   A Control App

Posted when a Session is closed by the user. In this case, the local control objects should delete themselves and their views. Closing a Session is not a distributed action, it should not affect other users.

ControlIndex

Inherits From: NSObject

Conforms To: NSObject (NSObject)
                    NSDraggingSource
                    NSNibAwaking
                    NSTableDataSource

Class Description

A ControlIndex is the control object for an Index object. It acts as the intermediary between its model, an instance of Index, and its interface objects (NSView and NSWindow objects created using Interface Builder).

A ControlIndex handles user actions such as opening and deleting agents. A ControlIndex is the target and receiver of action messages setup using Interface Builder—it is the owner of **ControlIndex.nib**.

These action methods update the state of the model to reflect changes made by the user.

Conversely, ControlIndex objects observe change notifications posted by their models and update their displays accordingly. For example, if a user changes the title of an agent, then all ControlIndex objects are notified and update their displays.

ControlIndex objects are also the delegates of their NSWindow objects and are notified before their windows are closed. The notification method **windowWillClose:** sends the **close:** message to the ControlApp instance, the delegate of NSApp. ControlApp's **close:** method allows the user to save changes to the index before closing.

ControlIndex objects are also notified when their models are about to be deleted, and since ControlIndex objects own themselves, they release themselves and close their windows (see **willDelete:**).

Adopted Protocols

NSDraggingSource	– draggingSourceOperationMask ForLocal:
	– ignoreModifierKeysWhile Dragging
NSNibAwaking	– awakeFromNib
NSTableDataSource	– numberOfRowsInTableView:
	– tableView: objectValueForTableColumn: row:

Method Types

Set and get methods	– model
	– setModel:
	– selectedAgents
	– window

Action messages	– open:
	– revert:
	– deleteAgents:
Index notifications	– indexDidChangeAgents:
	– willDelete:
Session notifications	– docDidChange:
NSTableView notifications	– selectionChanged:
NSWindow delegate messages	– windowWillClose:

Instance Methods

deleteAgents:

– (void)**deleteAgents:**(id)*sender*

Deletes the agents selected by the user from the receiver's model by sending it **delete**. Deleting an agent releases it as well as its control and interface objects by posting an ObjectWillDeleteNotification.

See also: – **willDelete:**

docDidChange:

– (void)**docDidChange:**(NSNotification *)*notification*

Invoked when the Session object changes the document in some way (as in a save or save as command). Updates the window to reflect the new document state and filename.

indexDidChangeAgents:

– (void)**indexDidChangeAgents:**(NSNotification *)*notification*

Invoked when the receiver's model changes its agents. Updates the table of agents and marks the window as "dirty."

model

– (id)**model**

Returns the receiver's model.

See also: – setModel:

open:

– (void)**open:**(id)*sender*

Opens the window corresponding to the selected agent.

See also: – selectedAgents

revert:

– (id)**revert:**(id)*sender*

Reloads the table of agents.

selectedAgents

– (NSArray *)**selectedAgents**

Returns the Agent objects that the user selected from the agents table.

See also: – open:

selectionChanged:

– (void)**selectionChanged:**(NSNotification *)*notification*

Invoked when the agents table selection changes, and updates the folder icon accordingly.

setModel:

– (void)**setModel:**(id)*anObject*

Sets the receiver's model to *anObject*. The receiver releases the old model if it exists and retains the new model (necessary when the model is remote). Adds itself as an observer of change notifications posted by the new model.

See also: – model

willDelete:

– (void)**willDelete:**(NSNotification *)*notification*

Invoked when the receiver's model is about to be deleted. Removes the receiver as an observer of remote notifications and releases it.

See also: – **windowWillClose:**

window

– (id)**window**

Returns the receiver's NSWindow object.

windowWillClose:

– (void)**windowWillClose:**(NSNotification *)*notification*

Invoked when the receiver's window is about to be closed. Sends **close:** to NSApp's delegate, a ControlApp object. The ControlApp object will perform a "clean" close operation by asking the user if he wants to same changes before closing. If the user confirms the close operation, the index will be deleted and this object, the receiver of this message, will be notified via **willDelete:**.

DistantNotificationCenter

Inherits From: NSNotificationCenter : NSObject

Conforms To: NSObject (NSObject)

Class Description

DistantNotificationCenter is a special notification center designed for Distributed Objects. DistantNotificationCenter, unlike NSNotification-Center, retains and releases remote observers. Remote observers are proxies that need to be retained—they are owned by their NSConnection objects and may be released when their NSConnection object is released. It is unpredictable when this might happen, and sending a

message to an invalid proxy raises an exception. Therefore, use Distant-
NotificationCenter instead of NSNotificationCenter if you expect remote
objects to add themselves as observers of notifications posted by local
objects.

In the Cards application, control objects observe remote entity object
notifications. Entity objects implement the **defaultCenter** method to
return an instance of DistantNotificationCenter, not NSNotification-
Center, by sending **defaultCenter** to the DistantNotificationCenter class
object. Control objects should send **defaultCenter** to their models when
adding themselves as observers of entity object notifications as in:

```
[[model defaultCenter]
    addObserver:self
    selector:@selector(agentDidChangeTitle:)
    name:AgentDidChangeTitleNotification
    object:model];
```

Similarly, control objects should remove themselves as observers from
the remote DistantNotificationCenter object before they are released.
Note, if you use NSNotificationCenter's **defaultCenter** method it will
return the local, NOT the remote notification center.

DistantNotificationCenter avoids dangling reference by simply overriding the primitive methods that add and remove observers. The observers are added to and removed from an array and therefore are retained
and released by the DistantNotificationCenter object. DistantNotificationCenter only retains remote observers once, no matter how many
times **addObserver:selector:name:object:** is invoked.

Method Types

Set and get methods	+ defaultCenter
Adding and removing observers	– addObserver:selector:name:object: – removeObserver:name:object:
Notification messages	– connectionDidDie:

Class Methods

defaultCenter

> \+ (NSNotificationCenter *)**defaultCenter**

Returns a shared DistantNotificationCenter if it exists, otherwise creates and returns a new instance of DistantNotificationCenter.

Instance Methods

addObserver:selector:name:object:

> – (void)**addObserver:**(id)*observer* **selector:**(SEL)*aSelector*
> **name:**(NSString *)*aName* **object:**(id)*anObject*

Retains *observer* if it's a remote object, then invokes the superclass implementation.

See also: – **addObserver:selector:name:object:**
(NSNotificationCenter), – **removeObserver:name:object:**

connectionDidDie:

> – (void)**connectionDidDie:**(NSNotification *)*notification*

Invoked when an NSConnection died. Releases all observers belonging to the dead NSConnection object.

removeObserver:name:object:

> – (void)**removeObserver:**(id)*observer* **name:**(NSString *)*aName*
> **object:**(id)*anObject*

Releases *observer* if it's a remote object, then invokes the superclass implementation.

See also: – **addObserver:selector:name:object:**,
– **removeObserver:name:object:** (NSNotificationCenter)

Index

Inherits From: NSObject

Conforms To: NSObject (NSObject)
NSCoding

Class Description

The Index object manages a lists of all the Agents and Author objects. Currently, the list of authors list only contains users that created agents belonging to the Index object—it is not a list of all users in the system. Index objects are entity objects that model persistent information. See the ControlIndex class specification for a description of an index's corresponding control and interface objects.

An Index object posts notifications whenever its list of agents changes (for example, an agent was added or removed, or the order changed), and when it is about to be deleted (see *Notifications*). Control objects observe these notifications and take appropriate action. For example, ControlIndex objects send **close:** to the ControlApp object (NSApp's delegate) when their models are deleted.

Adopted Protocols

NSCoding	– encodeWithCoder: – initWithCoder:

Method Types

Set and get methods	– agents – addAgent: – removeAgent: – authors – authorWithLogin: – defaultCenter
Notification methods	– agentDidChangeTitle: – agentDidChangeAuthor:

– agentDidChangeDate:
– agentDidChangeLock:
– willDelete:

Deleting an Index   – delete

Instance Methods

addAgent:

– (void)**addAgent:**(Agent *)*anAgent*

Adds *anAgent* to the receiver's agents, sorts them, and posts an Index-DidChangeAgentsNotification so that control objects can update their displays.

See also: – **agents**, – **removeAgent:**

agentDidChangeAuthor:

– (void)**agentDidChangeAuthor:**(NSNotification *)*notification*

Invoked when an agent's author changes. Posts an IndexDid-ChangeAgentsNotification so that control objects can update their displays (may be enhanced to optionally sort the agents by author names).

agentDidChangeDate:

– (void)**agentDidChangeDate:**(NSNotification *)*notification*

Invoked when an agent's modification date changes. Posts an IndexDid-ChangeAgentsNotification so that control objects can update their displays (may be enhanced to optionally sort the agents by modification date).

agentDidChangeLock:

– (void) **agentDidChangeLock:**(NSNotification*)*notification*

Invoked when an agent's lock state changes. Posts an IndexDid-ChangeAgentsNotification so that control objects can update their displays.

agentDidChangeTitle:

 – (void)**agentDidChangeTitle:**(NSNotification *)*notification*

Invoked when an agent's title changes. Sorts the receiver's agents alphabetically and posts an IndexDidChangeAgentsNotification so that control objects can update their displays.

agents

 – (NSArray *)**agents**

Returns the receiver's agents.

See also: – **addAgent:**, – **removeAgent:**

authors

 – (NSArray *)**authors**

Returns an array containing the receiver's Author objects.

See also: – **authorWithLogin**:

authorWithLogin:

 – (Author *)**authorWithLogin:**(NSString *)*login*

Returns the author corresponding to *login*.

See also: – **authors**

defaultCenter

 – (NSNotificationCenter *)**defaultCenter**

Returns the notification center that the receiver will use to post notifications. Use this method to observe notifications from the receiver.

See also: + **defaultCenter** (DistantNotificationCenter)

delete

– (void)**delete**

Posts an ObjectWillDeleteNotification so that control objects can take appropriate action.

removeAgent:

– (void)**removeAgent:**(Agent *)*anAgent*

Removes *anAgent* from the receiver's agents, sorts them, and posts an IndexDidChangeAgentsNotification so that control objects can update their displays.

See also: – **addAgent:**, – **agents**

willDelete:

– (void)**willDelete:**(NSNotification *)*notification*

Invoked when an agent is about to be deleted. Removes the notifying object, an Agent object, from the receiver using **removeAgent:**.

Notifications

IndexDidChangeAgentsNotification

Notification Object   An Index

Posted when an index's agents change. For example, agents were added or removed, or the order changed.

ObjectWillDeleteNotification

Notification Object   An Index

Posted when an Index object is about to be deleted.

Session

Inherits From: NSObject

Conforms To: NSObject (NSObject)
                        Session

Class Description

Session objects represent the shared workspace of a groupware session and manage information, such as the shared Index object and all its Agent objects. It also encapsulates the mechanisms used to store persistent objects (Index, Agent and Author objects).

Although a Session object is often remote (located in the CardsServer application), it can also be local. A local Session object does not behave any differently, it simply provides a common interface to the Cards application when no groupware session is active.

Most important, Session provides methods for creating Agent and Index objects. These methods should be used by clients instead of the typical **new:**, **alloc...** and **init...** methods. The **newAgent** method creates and returns a new Agent object that resides in the server process, NOT the client process. Similarly, **newIndex** creates an Index object for the Session object that resides in the server process.

If the Session object is remote, **setName:** can be used to change the password used to connect to the groupware session. Existing clients are not effected by the root object name change, but new clients need to use this new name to open a connection to the Session object. This mechanism allows a group of users to agree on a "password" for their session and excludes others from opening connections to their objects.

Session also contains methods for opening, saving, and closing documents. Currently, Session archives its Index object and consequently all the Agent and Author objects in files. Other than assuming a document-style interface, Session encapsulates the actual storage mechanism used. Methods could be added to Session to support other styles of persistent storage (for example, using EOF with a relational databases).

Method Types

Set and get methods	– index
	– setIndex:
	– newAgent
	– newIndex
	– defaultCenter
	– setName:
	– filename
	– setDocumentEdited:
	– is DocumentEdited
Persistency methods	– openFile:
	– saveFile:
	– closeFile:
Entity notifications	– docDidChange:

Instance Methods

closeFile:

  – (BOOL)**closeFile:**(NSString *)*fname*

Sets the index to **nil** using **setIndex:**. Returns NO if the index is already **nil**, YES otherwise.

See also: – **openFile:**, – **saveFile:**

defaultCenter

  – (NSNotificationCenter *)**defaultCenter**

Returns the notification center that the receiver will use to post notifications. Use this method to observe notifications from the receiver.

See also: + **defaultCenter** (DistantNotificationCenter)

docDidChange:

  – (void)**docDidChange:**(NSNotification *)*notification*

Invoked when an entity object changes its state in some way. Sets the document state to dirty and posts a SessionDidChangeDocNotification.

filename

– (NSString *)**filename**

Returns the filename the receiver uses to store the index.

index

– (id)**index**

Returns the receiver's Index object.

See also: **– newIndex, – setIndex:**

isDocumentEdited

– (BOOL)**isDocumentEdited**

Returns YES if the document was edited, NO otherwise.

See also: **– setDocumentEdited:**

newAgent

– (id)**newAgent**

Creates an Agent object and adds it to the receiver's Index. Returns the new agent. Clients should use this method not the **new:, alloc...** and **init...** methods when creating Agent objects.

newIndex

– (void)**newIndex**

Creates a new Index object by invoking **setIndex:** (releases the old index if it exists. Clients should use this method not the **new:, alloc...** and **init...** methods when creating Index objects.

See also: **– index, – setIndex:**

openFile:

– (BOOL)**openFile:**(NSString *)*fname*

Creates a new Index object for the receiver by opening and reading the contents of *fname*. If *fname* is **nil**, then the receiver's filename is used instead. Pass **nil** if you want to revert to the contents of the saved file. Returns YES if the operation was successful, NO otherwise.

See also: – **closeFile:**, – **saveFile:**

saveFile:

– (BOOL)**saveFile:**(NSString *)*fname*

Saves the receiver's Index object to the file specified by *fname*. If *fname* is **nil**, then the receiver's filename is used. Posts a SessionDidChangeDoc-Notification and returns YES if the operation was successful, otherwise returns NO.

See also: – **openFile:**, – **saveFile:**

setDocumentEdited:

– (void)**setDocumentEdited:**(BOOL)*flag*

If the flag is YES, marks the ControlIndex's window as "dirty" meaning it was edited by the user, otherwise marks it as "clean," not edited.

See also: – isDocumentEdited

setIndex:

– (void)**setIndex:**(id)*anIndex*

Sets the receiver's index to *anIndex*. Since the receiver owns its index, the old index is released and the new index is retained. Posts a SessionDid-ChangeIndexNotification.

See also: – **index**, – **newIndex**

setName:

– (BOOL)**setName:**(NSString *)*string*

Sets the receiver's name to *string* and changes the default NSConnection object's root name to *string* (assuming the receiver is the root object). This action has no effect on clients that are already connected to the receiver. However, clients forming new connections must use the new name. There is no method that returns the current name, so it is essentially private, known only by the participants. Returns YES if the operation was successful, NO otherwise.

Notifications

SessionDidChangeDocNotification

Notification Object   A Session

Posted when a Session object modifies its file (as in a save operation).

SessionDidChangeIndexNotification

Notification Object   A Session

Posted by **setIndex:** when a Session object's index changes.

Further Reading   E

Decline & Fall of the American Programmer

Edward Yourdon, *Decline & Fall of the American Programmer*, Prentice Hall, Englewood Cliffs, NJ, 1993.

Developing Business Applications with OpenStep

Nik Gervae and Peter Clark, *"Developing Business Applications with Open-Step,"* to be published by Springer-Verlag, 1996.

The Essential Distributed Objects Survival Guide

Robert Orfali, Dan Harkey, and Jeri Edwards, *The Essential Distributed Objects Survival Guide*, John Wiley & Sons, New York, NY, 1996.

Introducing Object-Oriented Technology into an Organization

Adele Goldberg and Kenneth Rubin, "Introducing Object-Oriented Technology into an Organization," ParcPlace Systems, 1990.

A Laboratory for Teaching Object-Oriented Thinking

Kent Beck and Ward Cunningham, "A Laboratory for Teaching Object-Oriented Thinking," *OOPSLA '89 Conference Proceedings, Special Issue of SIGPLAN Notices*, Volume 24, Number 10, October 1989.

No Silver Bullet Reconsidered

Brad Cox, "No Silver Bullet Reconsidered," *American Programmer Magazine*, November 1995.

The Object Advantage

Ivar Jacobson, Maria Ericsson and Agneta Jacobson, *The Object Advantage, Business Process Reengineering with Object Technology*, Addison-Wesley, Reading, MA, 1994.

Object Analysis and Design, Comparison of Methods

Andrew T. F. Hutt, *Object Analysis and Design, Comparison of Methods*, John Wiley & Sons, New York, NY, 1994.

Object Analysis and Design, Description of Methods

Andrew T. F. Hutt, *Object Analysis and Design, Description of Methods*, John Wiley & Sons, New York, NY, 1994.

Object Analysis and Design, Volume 1: Reference Model

Object Management Group, *Object Analysis and Design: Volume 1: Reference Model*, Draft 7.0, Object Management Group, Framingham, MA, 1992.

Object Behavior Analysis

Kenneth S. Rubin and Adele Goldberg, "Object Behavior Analysis," *Communications of the ACM*, Volume 35, Number 9, September, 1992. pp 48-62.

Object Lifecycles: Modeling the World in States

Sally Shlaer and Stephen J. Mellor, *Object Lifecycles: Modeling the World in States*, Yourdon Press, Englewood Cliffs, NJ, 1992.

Object-Oriented Analysis and Design with Applications

Grady Booch, *Object-Oriented Analysis and Design with Applications Second Edition*, The Benjamin/Cummings Publishing Company, Inc., Redwood City, CA, 1994.

Object-Oriented Design with Applications

Grady Booch, *Object-Oriented Design with Applications*, The Benjamin/Cummings Publishing Company, Inc., Redwood City, CA, 1991.

Object-Oriented Modeling and Design

James Rumbaugh, Michael Blaha, William Premerlani, Frederick Eddy, and William Lorensen, *Object-Oriented Modeling and Design*, Prentice Hall, Englewood Cliffs, NJ, 1991.

Object Oriented Programming: An Evolutionary Approach

Brad J. Cox, *Object Oriented Programming: An Evolutionary Approach*, Addison-Wesley, Reading, MA, 1986.

Object-Oriented Software Engineering

Ivar Jacobson, Magnus Christerson, Patrik Jonsson, and Gunnar Overgaard, *Object-Oriented Software Engineering*, Addison-Wesley, Reading, MA, 1992.

Object-Oriented Systems Design: An Integrated Approach

Edward Yourdon, *Object-Oriented Systems Design: An Integrated Approach*, Prentice Hall, Englewood Cliffs, NJ, 1994.

Objects—Born and Bred

Elizabeth Gibson, "Objects—Born and Bred," BYTE, October 1990, pp 245-254.

Software Engineering: Concepts and Techniques

Peter Naur, Brian Randell, and J.N. Buxton, *Software Engineering: Concepts and Techniques*, Mason/Charter, New York, 1976.

Succeeding with Objects: Decision Frameworks for Project Management

Adele Goldberg and Kenneth S. Rubin, *Succeeding with Objects: Decision Frameworks for Project Management*, Addison-Wesley, Reading, MA, 1995.

Testing Object-Oriented Components: A Human-centric Perspective

Brad Cox, "Testing Object-Oriented Components: A Human-centric Perspective," ACM, 1994.

Index